T0058034

ONE THOUSAND NIGHTS

AND COUNTING

ONE THOUSAND NIGHTS

AND COUNTING

* * * * * * * * * * *

SELECTED POEMS

* * * * * * * * * * *

GLYN MAXWELL

* * * * * * * * * * *

FARRAR STRAUS GIROUX

NEW YORK

FARRAR, STRAUS AND GIROUX
18 West 18th Street, New York 10011

Originally published in 2011 by Picador,
Published in the United States by Farrar, Straus and Giroux
First American edition, 2011

Grateful acknowledgement is made to the following publications, in which
some of these poems originally appeared: *Agenda, Agni, Atlantic Monthly,
Bostonia, Fulcrum, The Guardian, Illuminations, The Independent, The London
Review of Books, The Manhattan Review, Matrix, Metre, The New Criterion,
The New Republic, The New Yorker, The New York Sun, The Observer, Open
City, Oxford Poetry, The Paris Review, Ploughshares, Poetry, Poetry Review,
Poetry Wales, Poetry with an Edge* (Bloodaxe, 1988), *Rattapallax, The Rialto,
Sibila, Stand, The Sunday Times, The Times Literary Supplement, Trafika* and
Verse. The poems from *Phaeton and the Chariot of the Sun* were first published
in *After Ovid: New Metamorphoses*, ed. Michael Hofmann and James Lasdun
(Faber/FSG, 1994). 'Someone at the Door' was first published in
conjunction with the recording *Crye* by Concordia (Metronome, 1997).

All acknowledgements for permission to reprint
previously published material can be found on page 239.

Library of Congress Cataloging-in-Publication Data
Maxwell, Glyn, 1962–
    One thousand nights and counting : selected poems /
Glyn Maxwell. — 1st ed.
        p. cm.
    "Originally published in the United Kingdom in 2011 by Picador"—
T.p. verso.
    ISBN 978-0-374-53349-6 (cloth)
    I. Title.

PR6063.A869O54 2011
821'.914—dc22

                                                                2011005176

www.fsgbooks.com

IN MEMORY OF MY FRIEND

MATTHEW BURROWS

AND MY COUSIN

SIMON POWELL

CONTENTS

ONE THOUSAND NIGHTS

AND COUNTING

MY TURN

I have been so enchanted by the girls
who have a hunch, I have been seen

following them to the red and green
see-saws. There have been a few of them

I recognised. I have been recognised.
I have stood on the roundabout and turned.

I have swung, uselessly, not as high as them.
Then seen the parents coming, and the rain

on rusty and unmanned remaining things.
I have calculated west from the light cloud.

Cried myself dry and jumped
back on the roundabout when it had stopped.

Started it again, in the dark wet,
with my foot down, then both my feet on it.

JUST LIKE US

It will have to be sunny. It can rain only
when the very plot turns on pain or postponement,
the occasional funeral. Otherwise perfect.

It will have to be happy, at least eventually
though never-ending and never exactly.
Somebody must, at the long-last party,

veer to the side to remember, to focus.
All will always rise to a crisis,
meet to be shot for a magazine Christmas.

It will also be moral: mischief will prosper
on Monday and Thursday and seem successful
but Friday's the truth, apology, whispered

love or secret or utter forgiveness.
It will have to be us, white and faulty,
going about what we go about. Its

dark minorities will stay minorities,
tiny noble and gentle, minor
characters in more offbeat stories.

Its favourite couple will appear in our towns,
giving and smiling. Their tune will be known
by all from the lonely to the very young

and whistled and sung. It will all be repeated
once. Its stars will rise and leave,
escaping children, not in love,

and gleam for a while on the walls of girls,
of sarcastic students beyond their joke,
of some old dreadful untimely bloke.

It will have to be sunny, so these can marry,
so these can gossip and this forgive
and happily live, so if one should die

in this, the tear that lies in the credible
English eyes will be sweet, and smart
and be real as blood in the large blue heart

that beats as the credits rise, and the rain
falls to England. You will have to wait
for the sunny, the happy, the wed, the white. In

the meantime this and the garden wet
for the real, who left, or can't forget,
or never meant, or never met.

We passed, free citizens, between the gloves
of dark and costly cities, and our eyes
bewildered us with factories. We talked.

Of what? Of the bright dead in the old days,
often of them. Of the great coal-towns, coked
to death with scruffy accents. Of the leaves

whirled to shit again. Of the strikers sacked
and picking out a turkey with their wives.
Of boys crawling downstairs: we talked of those

but did this: drove to where the violet waves
push from the dark, light up, lash out to seize
their opposites, and curse to no effect.

THE ALBATROSS REVOLUTION

1

The Residence was coddled by the light
of albatrosses, many of them silent.

The summerhouse had had a green door then,
which banged and banged and shut, and the relevant

daughters of their Highnesses were to be seen
nowhere—probably putting on a play

or, at that flashpoint of the century,
heading somewhere new, reluctantly.

2

The albatrosses having flown inland,
the green door flew open. The daughters *and*

the friends they had were two groups that were not
there, and starlings were a small group that was,

though not for long. The lawn was wide and cold
with all these new commotions, and the sea

licked at the bony ankles of the cliff
as if it was their Highnesses. It rained.

3

Somebody laughed hysterically when
the full whiteness of the Residence

exposed itself to all—the random all
who shoved each other out of the forest now.

The starlings jabbed in the orangery.
The albatrosses did something different

elsewhere, the details quite available.
There was some sour cream in the Residence.

4

There were some bottles in the sea. The cliff
had stood ten centuries of them, and would,

to be honest, stand twenty centuries more.
Men climbed the chimneys of the Residence

even as podgy womenfolk exchanged
recipes involving cheese and sour cream.

And they flew flags, the men. And starling crap
made constellations on the cold wide lawn.

5

It rained. Whatever the flag meant, it sulked
or, at that flashpoint of the afternoon,

resulted in all sorts of things. The cream
was put to its sour use. The Residence

was multi-purpose, snaps of albatrosses
hung all about. The air grew dark and green

as uniforms, and, catapulting out
of a high window, the Albatross-Man.

FLOOD BEFORE AND AFTER

It reeled across the North, to the extent
that even Northerners cried 'This is North!'
and what would you have said, to see a sky

threatening the children with great change?
Extraordinary clouds! Spectaculars!
There was the Dimden family, in their barn.

And long, quite vertical rain, the three horizons
hunched, different formulations, browns
and oranges. Then the unlucky Greens

running with their sons to find their sons.
The scarecrow and the crow, they did okay,
getting dark together, but unfrightened.

Fists of clouds! Genii of glamour!
Not to mention thunders—not again!
There stand the Dimdens, safe for once and sad.

The Greens have found their sons! Now for their daughters.
But out goes the lightning, giant's fork
into a mound of chilli, steaming there

and where's it gone? Into the open mouth,
barn and all, flavours and seasonings!
Cuddle in the rain, old favourites.

There goes a Noah, borrowing a plank.
Little slow to move, we thought. It ends
with tangles, the new rivers, and the sunshine

formally requesting a rainbow. Granted.
The creaking and excusing back to work.
A valuable man was lost in it.

That was in the paper, with the picture.
All the Northern correspondents went
reading to the telephones, all cold,

which brought the dry onlookers from the South,
gaspers, whistlers, an ambassador
and leading lights to mingle with the hurt.

The clouds were diplomats of the same kind,
edging over to exonerate
and praise. And then the royal son arrived,

helicoptered down on a flat field,
glancing up at the sky through the whup of blades,
attending to the worried with a joke.

Hell, I don't know what—we were all cold.
The landscape looked an archipelago.
The Dimdens finally twigged, the Greens were found

beating the Blooms at rummy, in a cave.
All were interviewed and had lost all.
All saluted when the helicopter rose.

Only some came up the knoll with us
to check our options. Only two of those
saw, as I did, Noah's tiny boat

scarcely moving, at the edge of sight
below the line, and only I'd admit
the crow and the scarecrow were rowing it.

MATTERING

But the next day I was a hood with teeth,
and the red leaves were ankle-deep. Utter,
gaping memento mori to myself—
Alas! To cherish these things so—bobbing.

And this I memorised: if, in a yard,
you swear you see something, it's nothing but
another guileless chemical moment.—
When the bonfire-smoke mourned into the sky

forgetting murders, I was holding out:
my hands were these accomplishers, but blue,
distressed with what was animal in them

and wouldn't stop its mattering. 'Alas'—
an old word on an old cloud, like my God
when I was frowning at a picture book.

THE PURSUIT

Running through woods he came to the wrong wood,
the round wood. And he stopped there like a man
would in a sudden temple, and his own blood beat
on the cocked side, his hurt side, his red portside.

Running through trees like a deer, victimised,
a sprinter, of a minority, he passed
on into blacker greens and deep betweens,
lost to sight. We shrugged the Home County shrug.

'Running,' muttered those who report and wait:
'through woods,' added by them with a hunch and pencil:
'heart beating fast,' attested by the cadets:
'from here,' thrice-underlined by those from here,

he was seen. The relevant people looked for him,
I know, because their vans were parked on the rim
of the right wood, and they took their torches with them,
and left their maps and their furry animals hanging.

'Running through woods, heart beating fast, from here?
Let's go.' The reconstructed Xerox faces
appeared on walls from here to the uncrossable
M110, and it was said

the outer elms came back to life when the wire
linked them, to politely counsel *Don't*,
and in the ring of fire the rare and common,
darting, hopping, slithering, trudging, dragging

towards life-leasing coldness, from the smoke,
met in the heart of the wood and stared and were doomed.
It was said in the crackle and crack the stars went out.
The birds alone took life and the news away.

In the dry filth of the aftermath the drivers
found belongings, bagged and took them and waited.
Then radioed superiors on the rim.
But he ran elsewhere, though a red X was him.

The Mayor's son had options. One was death,
      and one a black and stylish trilby hat
he wore instead, when thinking this: I love.

The town was not elaborate. The sky
      was white collisions of no special interest
but look at the Mayor's son, at the bazaar!

'I've seen her once before . . .' Her name was this:
      Elizabeth. The Mayor's son was eighteen,
his mind older than that but his mouth not.

And had no options. 'Hey, Elizabeth!'
      I could say what was sold in the bazaar,
I could be clearer on the time of day,

I could define Elizabeth. I shall:
      every girl you ever wanted, but
can't have 'cause I do. She was twenty-one.

'Hi,—' the name of the Mayor's son? Anything.
      'Let's get something together!' someone said.
'The Mayor's son out with Lisa!' someone gossiped.

The afternoon, about to be misspent,
        stirred coffee with its three remaining fingers:
'They are sugar-crazy, they are milk-lovers

and they won't last.' Some things about the town:
        blue-printed in the days of brown and white
and laid down one fine evening, late July.

Musicians lived there, painters, people who
        did murders they'd mulled over, councillors
for other towns, golfers, golfers' widows,

widows of chip-eating carcasses
        dipping their chips and watching, wannabes
who are by now and has-beens who aren't yet,

people, ex-people, exes, seven mates
        of mine, no friends of yours, not you or me,
a footballer, a brothel-keeper, linesmen,

a Cabbage Patch Doll buying her own home,
        a band of Stuart Pretenders, a fire-hose
on a motorbike frequenting the one club,

and the man himself. No, strike him, he just left.
        Divide the town into eleven parts,
throw ten of them away and look at this:

they skated on the ice at the ice-rink,
        Elizabeth and a black-trilby'd boy
who kept his hat on. I'd have hated that

had I seen it. I hate hatted people who
        make such alert decisions to impress.
I'd have him on his arse. Oh good, he is.

Elizabeth, white-skirted (no more clues)
        swooped to sweep the Mayor's son off the ice
and pterodactyl-like he shook himself.

Hat elsewhere, kicked on by a small bully
        and ruined by that friend of his. Once
that would have shelled and reddened my idea,

to see such fun. But nowadays I just
        cram it in with all the other eggs
for omelette. Skate, skate, you're crap at it,

whatever your name is, you mayor's son.
        The Mayor's son and Elizabeth, oh my!
The middles of my afternoons in England.

Three simultaneous occurrences:
        a hump, a testimonial, a bomb.
Back to the ice-rink, just in time, we—

—There they are! Their two bicycles propped
         for vandals who'll show up in half an hour,
and off they go towards the library.

Conveniences everywhere, a town
         complete with detail, and the gardens so, so
green and tucked away! This is a poem

of love, whose hero had to urinate
         and did so, while Elizabeth began
to make a Christmas list, and left him out.

The air began to gather, *pointilliste*,
         and the early lamp went to a sorry pink
that wouldn't last, was a phenomenon.

They crossed roads, Beauty Gloved and the Mayor's son,
         they made split-second choices that saved lives.
The library was all a welcome cube.

The library was full of walruses.
         Or people who resembled walruses.
Or—no. The library was full of people

I'll never know. A man I'm calling Smith
         had borrowed Dante's *Purgatorio*
but not the other two. I had them both.

A man called Dorman had a book on trees,
          and it was lost and it had burned regardless
and it was ages overdue. A girl

who'd stripped the library of sailing books
          had drowned in any case and was so slow
to answer warnings that they'd phoned her up

to ask politely for their sailing books.
          A dictionary had gone missing too
but the Mayor's son had other things in mind!

How do we know? We don't, but he had options,
          and watched Elizabeth selecting books
on Archaeology, and choosing one

to look at and put back. The Mayor's boy
          nodded his head of ordinary hair
and felt love making soup with the utensils

he generally called his heart and soul.
          The sky was mauve, no other colour, mauve—
and I was splitting up with Alison.

I think it was that day, about half-six.
          The bully, meanwhile, read about a bike
and mentioned it to his belaboured dad

as a potential Christmas present. I—
        sometimes I hope he gets it, sometimes I
devoutly hope it kills him. Anyway

'the library is closing now'. The Mayor
        expected his son home. Elizabeth
expected that as well, didn't expect

what happened next as they waited for the cars
        to lose their nerve and stop. He put his hand
behind the head of this Elizabeth

and bruised her with a kiss, a mad one! He
        receded and she reappeared, a girl
with somebody to marry, and not him,

her mouth politicised indignity,
        her eyes becoming tyrants, *après-coup*:
'How dare you?' What a question. How dare you?

Because we don't know what—because we do—
        Irrelevant! Elizabeth was off.
The traffic-lights were either green or red—

I don't remember amber. The Mayor's son,
        no girl, no hat, beneath the sodium-
lamps of home. Oh hatchbacks of the time,

oh buses, oh pantechnicons! Next year
        the Mayor—who now eats fillets with his wife
and son, and fills a second glass with Soave

and tells a joke that no one gets—the Mayor
        will be deposed next year: his son will choose
a university, *it* will say no

to him but take Elizabeth, for Maths
        not Archaeology, and Alison
will suddenly, one day, in a Maths class,

befriend Elizabeth, and find their friends
        are mutual, like me and the Mayor's son,
who I'd never meet, and in a stand-up bar

all evening they'll be there. Meanwhile the books
        will pile up in my world, and someone's hat
will find its way to me and I will wear it.

We billion cheered.
      Some threat sank in the news and disappeared.
It did because
      Currencies danced and we forgot what it was.

It rose again.
      It rose and slid towards our shore and when
It got to it,
      It lined it like a telegram. We lit

Regular fires,
      But missed it oozing along irregular wires
Towards the Smoke.
      We missed it elbowing into the harmless joke

Or dreams of our
      Loves asleep in the cots where the dolls are.
We missed it how
      You miss an o'clock passing and miss *now*.

We missed it where
      You miss my writing of this and I miss you there.
We missed it through
      Our eyes, lenses, screen and angle of view.

We missed it though
        It specified where it was going to go,
And, when it does,
        The missing ones are ten-to-one to be us.

We walk the shore,
        Speak of the waving dead of a waving war.
And clap a man
        For an unveiled familiar new plan.

Don't forget.
        Nothing will start that hasn't started yet.
Don't forget
        It, its friend, its foe, and its opposite.

THE EATER

Top of the morning, Dogfood Family!
How's the chicken? How's the chicken?
Haven't you grown? Or *have* you grown,
here in the average kitchen at noontime
        down in the home, *at all*?

Bang outside, the bank officials
are conga-dancing in their pinstripe,
this is the life! But is it *your* life
out in the swarming city at crushhour
        dodging humans, *is it*?

Vacant city—where did they find that?
Blossom of litter as the only car
for a man goes by. When the man goes by
his girl will sullenly catch your eye:
        will you catch hers?

Snow-white shop—how do they do that?
Lamb-white medical knowing and gentle
sir, advise her, assure and ask her:
do you desire the best for your children
        and theirs? Well do you?

Take that journey, delight in chocolate,
you won't find anyone else in the world,
lady, only the man, the sweet man
opening doors and suggesting later
        something—what thing?

Short time no see, Dogfood Family!
How's the chicken? How's the chicken?
How have you done it? Have you done it
with love, regardless of time and income
        and me? Who am I?

I am the eater and I am the eater.
These are my seconds and these are my seconds.
Do you understand that? Do you get that,
you out there where the good things grow
        and rot? Or not?

SPORT STORY OF A WINNER

FOR ALUN

He was a great ambassador for the game.
                    He had a simple name.
His name was known in households other than ours.
                    But we knew other stars.
He could recall as many finalists
                    as many panellists.
But when they said this was his Waterloo,
                    we said it was ours too.

His native village claimed him as its own,
                    as did his native town,
adopted city and preferred retreat.
                    So did our own street.
When his brave back was up against the wall,
                    our televisions all
got us shouting, and that did the trick.
                    Pretty damn quick.

His colours were his secret, and his warm-up
                    rain-dance, and his time up
Flagfell in the Hook District, and his diet
                    of herbal ice, and his quiet

day-to-day existence, and his training,
                    and never once explaining
his secret was his secret too, and his book,
                    and what on earth he took

that meant-to-be-magic night in mid-November.
                    You must remember.
His game crumbled, he saw something somewhere.
                    He pointed over there.
The referees soothed him, had to hold things up.
                    The ribbons on the Cup
were all his colour, but the Romanoff
                    sadly tugged them off.

We saw it coming, didn't we. We knew
                    something he didn't know.
It wasn't the first time a lad was shown
                    basically bone.
Another one will come, and he'll do better.
                    I see him now—he'll set a
never-to-be-beaten time that'll last forever!
                    Won't he. Trevor?

PLAINT OF THE ELDER PRINCES

FOR DAVID

We are the first and second sons of kings.
We do the most incredibly stupid things.
      When we meet Elves
      We piss ourselves,
When we see adults walking around with wings

We crack up laughing and we take the mick.
We wind up in a cloud or we get sick,
      Or turned to stone
      Or wedding a crone
Or running widdershins and damned quick,

Or otherwise engaged, up to our eyes.
We brag, we stir, we mock and we tell lies.
      Upon our Quest
      Eight Kingdoms west
We find no peace: nobody evil dies.

No, seven Witches have a Ball and go to it.
Our sweethearts meet a toad and say hello to it.
      We bet it's our
      Brother De-ar:
It is, we ask a favour, he says no to it.

We are the first and second sons of queens.
We have our chances and our crucial scenes,
          But it comes up Tails
          While Our Kid scales
The castle walls with some wild strain of beans

To make his dream come out. What about ours?
We've wished on every one of the lucky stars:
          Got on with Wizards
          And off with Lizards,
Sung the gobbledegook to Arabian jars,

But no: we serve to do the right thing wrong,
Or do the bad thing first, or stagger along
          Until it's time
          For the grand old Rhyme
To drop and make our suffering its song.

The Fool implied that we were 'necessary'
In his last lay. This made us angry, very.
          Perhaps we are,
          But his guitar
Has found a lodging quite unsanitàry.

'Typical Them!' we hear them say at court:
'Brutal, selfish, arrogant, ill-taught!'
          They thought we would
          Turn out no good
And lo! We turned out just as they all thought,

We first and second Princes of the Blood.
Dreaming of a woman in a wood.
        Scaring the birds,
        Lost for words,
Weeds proliferating where we stood,

But hell, we have each other, and the beer.
Our good-for-nothing pals still gather here
        To booze and trample,
        A bad example
From which the Golden Boy can step or steer.

We're up, and it's a fine day in the land.
Apparently some Princess needs a hand.
        It's us she wants?
        Okay. This once.
Show us the map. This time we'll understand.

RUMPELSTILTSKIN

'Your name is Rumpelstiltskin!' cried
The Queen. 'It's not,' he lied. 'I lied
The time you heard me say it was.'
'I never heard you. It's a guess,'

She lied. He lied: 'My name is Zed.'
She told the truth: 'You're turning red,
Zed.' He said: 'That's not my name!'
'You're turning red though, all the same.'

'Liar!' he cried: 'I'm turning blue.'
And this was absolutely true.
And then he tore himself in two,
As liars tend to have to do.

OUT OF THE RAIN

I

The animals went in two by two, but I,
alive elsewhere, had been in the loudest town,

pleading. How do I start to explain to you
what was lost, and how, and even before

the rain that came and came?
Yes, it was fun in town. We've never denied

the length of the silver dresses, the babble and haze
of Friday nights and hell, even Sunday nights,

yes. I'd go into detail but I myself
was bright with it all and tended to misting over

if you see what I mean. My Ex was still around
then, but she wouldn't vouch for this, even if

she'd made it into the line herself, and she hadn't.
I hadn't either, and this—this is that story.

2

I do remember the last of the hottest days,
because Brack and I were picked to play for the Jungle.

He scored six and I was awarded the red.
Some of those lofty brothers played for the Town,

while their daddy hammered his embarrassing huge boat
on a day like that! The crowd would watch our match

then turn and laugh at the noise from the harbour. Ha!
Some of their people were out like that, in fact,

couldn't concentrate, and finally
conceded they couldn't win. Gallid walked

tensely to the platform for his shot,
and split the green to a three'er, and in a suit!

We linked our bats and danced to the Winners' Bar,
anxious for tall foaming Manzadinkas!

3

I know what you think: that meanwhile He held a trial
of thunderclouds and picked one blacker than black,

and patted its hair and said 'Go On, boy, Go Back
and Bring 'Em Hell!' but no, it was just our luck.

—The Weatherman, anyway, had said
the hot spell wouldn't hold, and of course why should it?

He showed us the LOWs, poised at the edge of the world,
the Weatherman, and he grinned and said, 'Good night.'

Then they showed our match! They did a feature
on Gallid, what an old star he was, and they say

they showed Brack and I, falling around on the lawn
some time after eleven. Lucky they did,

really, because we don't remember a thing.
We were out of our little skulls, in the jungle.

Before I finally—hell, and it's been a while—
tell about then, the end of the last dry night,

it's worth remembering what had been going on.
We'd had a shit-hot summer, that's for sure,

and the office guys were free to roll their sleeves
and booze or participate, or both, and they did.

There was a song that stayed top of the charts,
wouldn't fucking budge. It was called *I*

Want It Now—interesting thing about that:
they told me the tough little singer was last seen nude

and paddling through the studio, I mean really,
great video, or what? But her band were drowned.

What else—the Town won every bloody game
up to that day. I'm kind of proud of that.

The animals. Big question, yes, of course:
How did the mad prophetic son-of-a-bitch

find them all?—what's the word—the logistics.
Answer: haven't a clue. We did see lorries

parked on the slip road. There was that night with Coops
and my Ex, she was also Coops's Ex, creeping

up to the lorries and banging them and hearing
nothing. I mean, the hollow boom. So we thought

these had been left behind by some small firm
suddenly gone to hell. So we went home.

In retrospect they must have been full of insects.
And there were the quiet trains.

Haggit's kid kept saying in the morning
'There are trains all going by and no one hears them!'

You're starting to think: morons. But what was suspicious?
We assumed they were fuel trains, the secret ones,

and we weren't about to sully our hands with politics.
Anarchists, we weren't. Morons maybe.

But I haven't forgotten the buses.
Green, beige, pink and blue buses,

obsolete, used in the tourist season.
We thought—who wouldn't—the old crock was cashing in

like everybody else. I mean, old Haggit,
bless his last words ('You'll drown') was by that time

selling water, and Coops's surgery
was pay-as-you-enter, pay-as-you-stitch, and I

was preaching at a very slight profit.
All we thought was that he was doing what we were.

I'm trying to read the diaries I had
but it's all smudged, and I have to hum that song

to haul it back. Then there's a certain smell
fumes up that summer like nothing else on earth . . .

—Burning green leaves, his trees dying the death.
They tried to pass a law, you know, to stop him,

pretending they gave a toss about his woodland
when all they wanted to do was show him he couldn't

do what he wanted any more, because.
Because it was unnerving them, in the heat.

Because they didn't know why he was doing it.
Because, because. Because he was doing it.

They rushed it through. The Council hurried to stop
this outrage, as the last tree was lopped.

I suppose it's still on the statute-book in some
soaking hell. Where was I? In the jungle,

after the match. There was, I remember now,
a last-night-of-the-show feel to it all,

which I'd know about, as I was no slouch on the stage
either, and our production of *Gomorrah*

was banned at once and played to shrieking houses!
Me, I played the lawyer, my lines were

'Shut up, don't need to know' and 'No, you can't'
and—can't remember, something about a warrant.

Coops was a headless king, my Ex his widow,
and Haggit played himself but not very well.

Good days. But yes, it did feel a bit, you know,
like, what the hell would there be to do tomorrow?

In the Winners' Bar there'd been Olde Tyme Oyle,
there'd been Manzadinka by the gallon, Chuice,

Diet Light, pints and pints of Splash,
and all the usual girls between the curtains.

There'd been songs of winning, anthems of the Jungle
Club, there'd been speeches and falling down,

and taunts and chants directed at the Town!
I mean it was quite a night, and I've asked myself:

what the hell did we head to the jungle for?
There was Brack and I, Haggit, the blue winger,

the mascot with his mushrooms, and some girl.
We'd most of us played for the Jungle, but so what?

It didn't mean we came from there, although
the winger did—and that girl, and in fact the mascot.

Funny how all in the space of what was maybe
half an hour, everything that was starting

clearly announced it was starting. There was a rumble.
There was a vast boomerang of birds

black against the black-green of the jungle's
drenched sky: there was a second, different rumble.

We had a debate. We were always having debates.
Even out of our tiny heads, we were picking

fair sides to wonder what the hell
the rumbles were, and how far away they were.

The junglies—Brack was calling them that
and right to their little faces—the junglies all

got nervous. The winger, who'd not touched a drop, was sure
the war was starting—'Or at least two different wars!'

The girl, who'd arrived with somebody nobody knew
and had lost him, or just left him with his drink,

made to speak, but so did Haggit. Then
the girl said, 'N-n-no, it's a great

elephant larger than any town!' The mascot
gulped and seconded that, but said it was green.

Then Haggit scoffed, and Brack said, 'That's no elephant,'
as a third rumble came, 'That's my mother!'

And so it was left to me to feel the cold,
and calm them down. 'Sod it, it's just thunder.'

Full marks for irony, of course, but remember,
it had been a good nine months. Then Haggit and Brack

got serious and agreed. Which meant the junglies
were outvoted, as the girl had disappeared.

More obviousnesses then. Sheet lightning.
God's face on it, bored, on His chin.

One of us shouting, 'Knock it off!' to Him.
And suddenly it stopping, at our shins.

'Ahem, let's go home,' ventured Haggit,
wobbling on a log. 'We'll get a chill.'

And we asked the blue winger, who in our game
had played what they call a blinder, to help out

for teammates' sakes, by showing us our way.
Brack was getting jumpy. 'What do you say?

Will you help us out, us three?'
It was very dark. He was speaking to a tree.

'Fucking fairweather friend,' he spat. 'Blue freak!'
And the mascot giggled and we were up shit creek.

No wonder Brack was losing it: after all,
he was a news-hound, that was what he did.

They'd be screeching for him, threatening his friends
back in the newsroom—'Where's Brack? IT RAINED!'

He could hardly call in sick, after his great
heroics in the match, and his face in the News:

so he knew he was out of a job.
No of course he didn't know we all were.

Haggit, meanwhile, he had a wife and kid,
who'd certainly be waiting to be angry.

But he was a calm kind of man, and he said,
'Let's work it out from the light.' I said, 'What light?'

I do admit I was hardly a help. I kept thinking
of the losers happy in the Winners' Bar, drinking.

We waded where we thought we'd waded from.
We couldn't lose the mascot, who kept saying,

'Whistlework, whistlework,' and our only
guide was the one cloud pierced

by the moon, and only at times.
Otherwise it was dark and the only sounds

were the mascot and, ultimately, Brack
drowning it. Then we were worried men

and cold, thinking of lawns and admitting it.
We waded on, it got drier, higher up,

a good sign, for our port was on a hill.
That's why they called us mad, but we didn't choose

to have the sea up there, where the ancient bloke
had made his boat, and we called him mad too.

They called us—not only mad—wait for it,
the Golden Generation. It was our cars,

and our carefree times, our drinks on the roofs of homes,
our tilted velvet hats in the winter, our games

and how we used our leisure, made it work for us,
our softness on ourselves, our relaxed

attitude to money. Most of all,
because we called ourselves Golden. And hell,

good times. But as I say—that last-night air:
what would there be to do tomorrow? More.

More of the gazing over the black-tiled floor
for that single someone, more of the same jazz

in all four corners of the cars, and more
seasons of the League, and those hot days.

We were near the shore. We knew that by the smell
of salt and gull, and sometimes the sound

of breakers but Haggit shrugged and said, 'Thunder.'
I didn't think so. Brack

seemed to snag his ankle on each tree
like he was trying to, and the moon came right

out, and we caught each other's eyes. 'Right,'
said Brack: 'this is a nightmare. Pinch my cheek.'

I closed my eyes, while Haggit lost his temper,
and so it was I who heard them—girls' voices.

Drunk as us, drunker than us, moving
towards us not away from us, and many:

Brack said 'This is a dream. Leave me alone.'
Haggit and I just stood. We were shaking.

A second's realisation of torchlight.
A second second's seeing we were found . . .

'Hoo, trolls! Look who's been in the rain!
Ahoo, aha! A treasury of wet men!'

'Is it really them?' 'Is it really who?' 'No!
It isn't them, it's men!' 'Where was the party,

and what were you?' There were six or seven of them,
they had cloaks, they were on their way from something, I

actually thought I knew a couple. Anyway,
they were townspeople all right, and I breathed again.

Brack was talking about our match, our win,
and our looking for fun, but Haggit was squatting down

a misery in the water. One girl said,
'Did you hear the wars? Did you hear the elephants?'

The wind blew. Another girl said this:
'We're swimming out to the Island for tonight!

There's your fun, heroes! Nobody's there
at this time, and we've got some hammocks there

and Manzadinka, yay! out on the Island,
and then in the morning we swim home to sleep.'

I'm not telling you this because they all
died out there—of course they did, they woke

and there wasn't land—I'm telling you why
it sounded such fun, and Brack said, 'Come on!'

and went with them. It's not like he was mad
or irresponsible, I mean, he was,

but he'd lost his job by then, and he had no kids
or wives to speak of. I had to stay with Haggit.

Then there's a blank time—
Haggit had stopped talking, or when he did

he was talking to Brack, and I said, 'He isn't there'
but it's very vague, though I do remember the girls

in their blowing firelight, trying to lure us
into the woods to change our minds, then suddenly

running away in silence. Then the wind
colossal in the trees, and drops again.

All those trees, all those millions of trees.
Could've come in handy. Wish I'd been

elected, in on it, if you know what I mean—
rather than what I was, the last to make it

out of the sea, the miracle in wet clothes.
Swearing oaths.

The animals went in two by two, I saw them—
later, later, after the girls and the lightning

illuminating the black ocean and figures
swimming out to the shrinking island, after

the still mascot, after the rain resuming,
and the last dry inch of my body, and Haggit's

wild decision to climb to the top of a pine:
'What are you doing? Come down, come down, come down!' 'I'm

staying here till it's over, son. I can see
hundreds of clouds coming. I don't see the town.

Stay on the earth if you have to, but you'll drown!'
'I won't!' 'You will!' 'I won't!' Well I won't rub it in,

but when the wall of water broke the spit
it would have swamped those pines in about a minute—

but after I started to run, later, I saw them:
I must have been some way inland,

where the country rose again and rather than wading
I splashed through groves and glades—but it was

amazing—a dry risen corridor of light
guarded (I crouched and shook) through which in, yes,

yawn, yawn, in pairs, the animals went,
some still sleeping, some complaining,

one or two reading, others crying,
others terrified by the mauve heavens

or pointing out God to friends who knew it was Him,
I mean who else would show Himself at a time

like this? But it was just a cloud
and it split in half.

I backed away, and the light drummed on my back
as I ran and ran and just as I decided

to say a prayer before I died, I tripped
and collided with a stone—or with a square.

I had a square in my mind when I blacked out,
and a square in front of me when I was choked

awake by the water rising. It was a garden
path stone, the first of thirty stones

zigzagging up to a door where a Unicorn
asked me the last animals I saw.

'I saw two Zebras. Following two Yaks.'
'What's your name?' the Unicorn wondered.

I gave it. 'Ah, then you missed your place in the queue.
Like us. But we were always going to.'

23

And these in my dazed state were only words,
though you see they stuck. I blinked, and felt

my whole frame lifted on to a warmth
of animal, white, white animal,

—did I say Unicorn? Yes,
a Unicorn, and it was bearing me

out of the rain, into a room of lamps
and beating lives all blurring into a focus.

They were all animals I hadn't seen,
and never did again, though I saw them now.

They all resembled what I knew, but either
thinner, gentler, slower, or a new colour

and I sat in a ring with them whatever they were,
and the Unicorn sat opposite, and said these words . . .

'One day they came and took the Cat, who'd lied.
They left behind the Other, who'd said nothing.

They came again, and took the eating Dog,
while the Other stopped and offered his food, and stared.

They came again, and fooled the Elephant
who wanted to be fooled; the Other didn't.

They took the Fox next, who seemed reluctant,
and told the Other, "You stay here on watch."

They took the Jackdaw who was screaming, "I!"
which left the Other, quiet, making a nest.

No problem for the righteous Lion: he went,
but the Other was troubled, needed time to think.

When they next came, the Monkey had packed a case,
but the Other, puzzled, had nothing to put in a case.

Then the Natterjack, told he'd meet a Princess,
leapt in the air, but the Other fell about.

The Owl put down his book, said, "I deserve",
and told the Other, "I find you don't deserve."

The Pig—you should have seen him—he almost flew!
But the Other couldn't, so wouldn't, but still hopes to.

The Shark was next—and you know this trip was free?
—he paid a million; the Other said, "Not me."

The Sheep were hard to separate, but one
went with the ones who went, and the Other stayed

with the ones who stayed. The Snake was next, accusing
the Other so silently he never knew

why he was left behind with the likes of me
and the Other Unicorn, who stayed with me.'

And who then came in with towels, which reminded me:
'Why one at a time? I saw double that.'

Which made her laugh. 'We saw you on the news,
we know about your escapades!—but listen:

are you just a drunken Man—or part of the business?
Who were the ones who went?' 'Nobody went

anywhere!' I cried, 'It was just raining!
There'll be a hell of a lot of mud in the morning!

—but nobody died, did they? What are you saying?'
'Oh,' said a huge bird sadly,

'has anyone been doing something odd
recently, in your town? Like, building something?'

'Only the man with the planks, this local git,
building a sort of—big . . . oh holy shit.'

I suppose I overreacted. The lines were down
anyway, and the lights were packing in.

They put me to bed a while, which I shared with something
not unlike a Woman, but comprehensible

and with one face. I couldn't sleep. The rain
never let up, and I went downstairs again.

Some of the furrier guests were thinking
of turning in by then, but things like bats,

otters, hedgehogs—brighter colours, though—
began to reminisce, just wouldn't go,

and the mousy thing in the coat just stared and stared
out of the window.

I ended the night at chess with the bored Yeti.
'Did your companion go?' I asked. 'Dunno.'

I must have got my second wind then,
as the next thing I remember is a full

harmonious hum of snoring, in the dark,
ranging from the unhearable to the zurr

of a bearish group in the library, and always
the rain and as I left,

as I stood on the WELCOME mat and said my quiet
'So long' to the left behind, and left them,

and ventured out to the light and the first stone,
I saw an extraordinary thing—I mean,

even by these standards—how the whole
garden and cottage, seething with the asleep,

was a deep deep hole in the sea, and all around
the walls of water poured against the ground!

Nobody was disturbed but I—I saw
water, white with fury at this Law,

fall and fountain again, against its will,
leaving us dry and pocketed, a well

of oxygen in what was the end of a world.
The greenness here, the life of it, was so strong

I thought, 'Nobody's wrong, nothing's wrong,'
and it felt like my first thought, and I felt how the grass

stayed bone dry to the last.
I thought of waking the Unicorns, and just as I

thought to myself, 'There are no such things
as unicorns,' the water spurted out

and gripped my feet and whirled me up this spout
up onto the flat sea and that was that.

Day, I guess. The sky was a sagging grey.
Everywhere dead land and debris,

and after swimming in turn to three of the four
horizons of the dome,

I twisted to look at the last, and it had to be home.
Home, though it shouldn't have been, was a high

ridge with its back to the sea,
and the rain would have to have filled the valley before

the town would flood, although by then
it would have done, and had.

So what were left were the roofs, and the high arena
where we did our plays, and also the Heroes Tower

which from these miles seemed swollen at its steeple
like a hornets' nest on a stick. Clinging people.

I swam, and thought of the dead. I thought, 'They're dead.'
(I was known as a thinker at school, I'll have you know.)

I thought of the things I'd seen, and thought, 'I didn't
see those things.' (I was known as a liar, too.)

I swam over trees and everything I had once
run through, and it all seemed much simpler

and, feeling my confidence build, I stood on the water,
which didn't take my weight. I sank, I swam.

It began to rain again, and had always rained.
I imagined the Winners' Bar an aquarium.

Which made me think of the match, which led to the thought
of the noise of the hammering father in his harbour,

which led me to scan the horizon
for his boat and zoo, but no, they were gone like him—

—to the Dry, the Saved, the Impossibly Full: a book.
Good end for all that wood, I thought, blankly.

Then I caught some floating door
and lay on it, closed my eyes and trusted it:

I would float upsea to the town.
And we floated upsea to the town.

What was left of it, well yes, we've all seen pictures,
but it's really only another view, only

the dead are about and prices have fallen down,
there's no sport played for a while, and the Police

are pally, or warn and fire. Charities come,
and interviewers and the place becomes

famous. But—hell, famous for whom?
Well, okay. Nobody this time.

33

Washed in, I was reckoned dead. When I woke again
I was on dry land on a roof with the whole Council.

In fact I disturbed a debate on the recent crisis,
and the Mayor, about to cast his casting vote,

nulled and voided the meeting. All my fault.
They adjourned to look at the view, and as I crawled

and stumbled back to an upright position, an old
stalwart took me aside and told me, 'Oh

what a great debate it was!
Some insist we're afloat on a floating detached

roof, others that this is the one building
left, i.e. we've been chosen above all

not to, er, and so on.' 'How did you vote?'
'Oh come on, secret ballot, sir, and all that.'

And then I saw all eyes were on me, the one
neither dead, nor drowning, nor on the Council.

So I said, 'Here you are—where are the real people?'
A hushed hiatus then, but the Mayor said, 'There,

there,' and I told him to stuff his sympathy,
but he pointed at where the Tower had been and where

it now was, a rolling log that couldn't
help any of the hundreds trying to grip it

and splashing to matey death, in each other's way.
The Mayor sat down with me,

and they say I suddenly lost it and screamed at him
to go to the house in the wood and help them in,

and find the lot in the boat and scuttle them!
The Mayor looked at his watch: 'Gentlemen,

Time is immaterial. We have
a roof, we have about two dozen men,

we have the bust of the founder, which is round . . .
I reckon that just about makes a troppling ground!'

And so they played and I looked out to the sea,
and the sea and the dead, the drowning, the dead and the sea,

and then I joined in a while and managed a five-o
before losing out to the Mace-Man's cunning yellow.

'Ha! Not looking, were you?' The Mace-Man roared,
as the rain from heaven pissed on our troppling board.

'It's slackening off,' a fielder said. He seemed
curiously blue for a town official,

but hell he was right about that, and the Weatherman stared
up at the sky, and said, 'I want to bat.'

By the time we reached half-time the air was only
dirty, a muzzy brown, like a sand but nothing.

The rain was hardly rain, more like a reminder.
The level remained level. The sea was headless.

We were winning 16–9 with a red in the bucket.
I was always, always going to say, 'Oh, fuck it,'

as I walked and dived and swam and looked back only
to see a half-mile away

the prizes passing from Mayor to Man, and the caps
thrown in the air and to hear,

small on the wind like the smell of men, 'hooray!'
and then a silence, then

'hooray', tinier than can be, and then
'hooray', and silence. Nothing. This is me.

I was born where I knew no man, nor that
the rain would fall, nor end, nor that a boat

would sail away and none that I knew would follow.
All that I knew are gone, and all

that I know I love and is here and knows it will not
know me tomorrow.

I was born, I know, in a town which never
should have been built where it was, but was,

and I live in this same one next to the sea
where nothing changes but is.

But is that one cloud ever going
to move again, as I bat and believe

it will, or is that the sentence passed?
Time has gone, townspeople, townspeople, time is lost.

I've been working on this page,
for an age, in the sun.

I'll move towards the open window,
place my hands in the sun.

I'll stroll out to the match where we are
winning it in the sun.

We are two points clear in every league there is.
Bar none.

I'll stroll back from the match where we are
coasting home in the sun.

I'll see my Ex through the open window or
someone, tanned in the sun.

We'll love and laugh and win at all we do.
Or have done.

'Yes, well I'm an authority on history,'
I tell the eight reserves when I meet them

in the Winners' Bar, taking the daily pictures
of one of only how many survivors?

They ask me, but I shake my head: 'No questions!'
They think I'm joking and they shake my hand.

I give a boy an autograph. I gave him it
yesterday. I'll give him it tomorrow.

I wonder what he thinks of me. The Weatherman
goes past. He's out of a job. I say I'm sorry.

Two of the Council, Gingham and Sub-Gingham,
always mention unicorns when they pass me.

They think that's funny. Gennit, the matchwinner,
shuts them up with a look. And goes past me.

Guess what I saw. 'Your Ex? And she was standing
out on the pitch and waving, wearing a silk

she cut with your own money? And she so wanted
you to go up, so you did,

and she spoke in a new way and her silk came down
and all that was there was yours and you married in town!

Am I right? Oh I'm sorry.
What did you see?' Forget it. Don't worry.

The game is starting now, anyway.
Shall we go and see that game? If we win

we'll be two points clear. So I hope we win. If we win
let's go to the Winners' Bar, I've a seat there. 'Yeah?

What's your poison?' Manzadinka.
Manzadinka! 'What?' Manzadinka!

I can see you through this glass,
all of you. Go on, guess, guess,

guess what I saw. No, a weather forecast.
I'm telling you the truth. It was illegal

but they let it happen. 'Oh.' Is that what you say?
Oh? Yes, I overheard it happen.

'And.' Is that what you say?
And? Is that all? Well. And nothing.

Still the same. Yes, you're dead right I'm mad.
I could see you through the glass, you had a horn

and so did he, you were making fun of me.
But tell them, Mr Councillor, who scored

the Double-Green that day, when the Town were out
for two pinks and a fifty—tell them that!

I wake in a hot morning, and I make
a breakfast for a man who needs a breakfast!

Nothing has changed. I warm the last night coffee
and reread the local paper where it says

we won and we are two points clear. The sun
is high above my home. Nothing has moved.

We're favourites for the match today. But don't think
for a moment we won't try.

I hope my Ex will phone. I mow the lawn.
I lecture. I once saw a Unicorn.

No, two. I turn my personal radio on.
I Want It Now has gone to Number One.

I finish this and put it on the shelf.
I take it down and send it to myself.

HELENE AND HELOISE

So swim in the embassy pool in a tinkling breeze
The sisters, *mes cousines*, they are blonde-haired
      Helene and Heloise,
One for the fifth time up to the diving board,
The other, in her quiet shut-eye sidestroke
Slowly away from me though I sip and look.

From in the palace of shades, inscrutable, cool,
I watch exactly what I want to watch
      From by this swimming pool,
Helene's shimmer and moss of a costume, each
Soaking pony-tailing of the dark
And light mane of the littler one as they walk;

And the splash that bottles my whole life to today,
The spray fanning to dry on the porous sides,
      What these breathtakers say
In their, which is my, language but their words:
These are the shots the sun could fire and fires,
Is paid and drapes across the stretching years.

Now Heloise will dive, the delicate slimmer,
Calling Helene to turn who turns to see
      One disappearing swimmer
Only and nods, leans languorously away
To prop on the sides before me and cup her wet
Face before me near where I'd pictured it.

I was about to say I barely know them.—
I turn away because and hear of course
            Her push away. I see them
In my rose grotto of thought, and it's not a guess,
How they are, out of the water, out
In the International School they lie about,

What they can buy in the town, or the only quarters
Blondes can be seen alighting in, and only
            As guided shaded daughters
Into an acre of lonely shop. 'Lonely?'
Who told me this had told me: 'They have no lives.
They will be children. Then they will be wives.'

Helene shrieks and is sorry—I don't think—my
Ankles cool with the splash of her sister's dive:
            I wave and smile and sigh.
And so goes on the fall of a man alive,
And twenty-five, and the wetness and the brown
Hairs of my shin can agree, and I settle down.

'Already the eldest—suddenly—the problems.
The other scribbles faces.' I had heard
            Staccato horrid tantrums
Between earshot and the doorbell, held and read
Heloise's letters in chancery
Script to her dead grandmother, to me,

To nobody. They have a mother and father,
And love the largest pandas in the whole
   World of Toys. The other
Sister rang from Italy and was well,
But wouldn't come this time. 'She'll never come.
She has a home. They do not have a home.

Stretching out in her shiny gold from the pool,
Heloise swivels, and sits and kicks
   Then reaches back to towel
Her skinny shoulders tanned in a U of lux-
Uriant material. Helene
Goes slowly to the board, and hops again

Into the dazzle and splosh and the quiet. Say,
Two, three miles from here there are heaps of what,
   Living things, decay,
The blind and inoculated dead, and a squad
Of coldly infuriated eyeing sons
Kicking the screaming oath out of anyone's.

Cauchemar.—We will be clear if of course apart,
To London again, me, they to their next
   Exotic important spot,
Their chink and pace of Gloucestershire, Surrey, fixed
Into the jungles, ports or the petrol deserts.
I try but don't see another of these visits,

As I see Helene drying, Heloise dry,
The dark unavoidable servant seeming to have
        Some urgency today
And my book blank in my hands. What I can love
I love encircled, trapped, and I love free.
That happens to, and happen to be, me,

But this is something else. Outside the fence,
It could—it's the opposite—be a paradise
        Peopled with innocents,
Each endowed with a light inimitable voice,
Fruit abundant, guns like dragons and giants
Disbelieved, sheer tolerance a science—

Still, I'd think of Helene, of Heloise,
Moving harmless, shieldless into a dull
        And dangerous hot breeze,
With nothing but hopes to please, delight, fulfil
Some male as desperate and as foul as this is,
Who'd not hurt them for all their limited kisses.

Sometimes only the ginger-haired in Heaven
can help me with my life. The flock of blondes
is sailing by so painlessly forgiven,
still blinking with love no one understands,

while the brunettes float thinking by the rushes
long after what they chose, long reconciled,
and here, the fair and sandy, all their wishes
half-granted them, half-wish them on a child.

Only the ginger-haired remember this, though:
this sulk and temper in the school of time,
this speckled hope and shyness at a window
as sunlight beats and blames and beckons. I'm

not coming out. They won't come out of Heaven,
or not until with auburn in the blood
two mortal tempers melt together. Even
then we might stay here if you said we could.

First day of school. A boy looks through a pane.
This is the end of freedom, not a visit.
The King's Cross–York–Newcastle–Scotland train
Slams through Welwyn Garden and I miss it.

*

1880. This asthmatic geezer
Home from Nebraska batters down a map.
Says Bernard Shaw, 'What's that there, Ebenezer?'
'Hush,' says Howard, 'I think I've found a gap.'

*

Woods were north. The south was all my schools.
East was alien housing, west I knew.
Start of a poet. All the rest is false
Or true extrapolations of the view.

*

A MARTIAN VOTES IN WELWYN-HATFIELD

Inhabitants converge upon a shed
One by one all day, to make a cross.
Outside their homes some show their feelings: red
For really cross, yellow for fairly cross.

*

Before the night begins, my friend and I
Stop outside the autobank. I run
To take out forty quid. We drive away.
'Out stealing from yourself again, eh Glyn?'

*

They lost their nerve in 1970.
'It's neither Welwyn, a garden, nor a city.'
They thought up 'Howardstown' and 'Waverley'
Since nothing had these names and they were pretty.

*

Western Garden Citizen, I stand
At midnight in the east and say, 'I'm lost.'
But I'm starting to get to know the back of my hand,
At the cost of moving on, which is no cost.

*

Small hours. The tots are in their cots. The old
Are in their homes. The thin Nabisco towers
Snore the malt. Two strangers have and hold,
And, as in real places, something flowers.

*

Who's in the kitchen? London, the life and soul
You weary of, flirtatious, loud, and hot.
A young well-meaning man is in the hall.
He's got his gift and bottle. What have you got?

INVIGILATION

There was barely a one among them who thought he needed
The three whole hours allowed. After say two,
Big papers started to bloom. I went out to collect them.

Divested of their petals the candidates each
Sank back dead with a sigh and the clock went suddenly
Still, unsure who was asking what, so it just

Went if they weren't looking, and not if they were.
I, having cruised this test in another life,
Saw rhombuses in my name and coloured them in.

Until as there always is there was only one,
One in the light, on the spot, while the rest of them stared
In exasperation escalating to anger,

Not that after their answers a slower answer
Was worming across a space, but that that answer
Was nudging the world and it was too late to right it.

LOVE MADE YEAH

First and zillionth my eyes meet eyes
       unturnable from, unstarable in.
Whoever was marched from the Square of my reason
and to what court, I don't give a hyphen,
       va t'en to the King!

Our drapeaux are waving and what's in the offing
       but tears, tribunals and unwelcome aid?
Nothing but glorious, jealous, incredulous,
bibulous, fabulous, devil'll envy us
       love made, love made!

'Yeah,' but you'll say, with the press of the planet,
       'Look how it turns out: the heroes felled
in the upshot, the oiliest climb of the customary
bourgeois fuckers as easy as muttering
       argent, ackers, geld . . .'

Uh-huh, sans doute. But here at the heart
       of the movement I trust my hand in another!
So CNN tells me I'm odds-on to cop it?
That ain't news, guys, I did arrive here
       via a mother.

No, when the Square is still again, but
        for some oligarchy or puppet or shah,
and I'm banged up and on trial in slippers
for following, wishing on, crediting, catching
        her my star—

don't do the pity. All right, do the pity,
        but that won't happen, believe it from me!
Her eyes are as hot as one needs to ignite
the cave in the human guy. I am hers,
        friends, I am history!

STARGAZING

The night is fine and dry. It falls and spreads
the cold sky with a million opposites
that, for a moment, seem like a million souls
and soon, none, and then, for what seems a long time,
one. Then of course it spins. What is better to do
than string out over the infinite dead spaces
the ancient beasts and spearmen of the human
mind, and, if not the real ones, new ones?

But, try making them clear to one you love—
whoever is standing by you is one you love
when pinioned by the stars—you will find it quite
impossible, but like her more for thinking
she sees that constellation.

After the wave of pain, you will turn to her
and, in an instant, change the universe
to a sky you were glad you came outside to see.

This is the act of all the descended gods
of every age and creed: to weary of all
that never ends, to take a human hand
and go back into the house.

WATCHING OVER

Elated by ourselves, we shift and slip—
Mouths open with the memory of a kiss—
Parting in two for sleep, and if it's mine

Then that was it, that break above, and now
It's yours I wake to witness your unknowing
Our time and all you know.
                            Some ancient will,
Though night is safe and quiet here, commands
You be watched over now, and, to that end,
Exacerbates the wind and whipping rains,
Or amplifies the howls of animals
To make my waking watchful and tense,
Though for a thousand miles there is no mind
To hurt you, nor one raindrop on the wind.

THE SENTENCE

Lied to like a judge I stepped down.
My court cleared to the shrieks of the set free.
I know the truth, I know its level sound.
It didn't speak, or didn't speak to me.

The jury got the point of her bright look,
The ushers smoothed her path and bowed aside,
The lawyers watched her fingers as she took
Three solemn vows, her lipstick as she lied.

She vowed and lied to me and won her case.
I'm glad she won. I wouldn't have had her led
However gently into the shrunken space
I'd opened for her. There. There now it's said,

Said in this chamber where I sleep of old,
Alone with books and sprawling robes and scent.
With all I have, I have no power to hold
The innocent or the found innocent.

EITHER

A northern hill aghast with weather
Scolds and lets me hurry over.
Someone phoned to tell my father
Someone died this morning of a
Stroke. The news has tapped me with a
Stick. I vaguely knew his brother.
No one knows where *I* am either.

Now I'm lost. I don't know whether
This road runs along the river
Far enough. I miss my lover,
Town and all the south. I'd rather
Die than be away forever,
What's the difference. Here's another
Field I don't remember either.

THE MARGIT-ISLE

FOR PATRICK HOWARTH

The boy had died. We knew that right away.
'Es gibt kein Luft,' I said. On a cold day
We should have seen his breath as a cone of mist.
I was proud I'd used some German words. We stood
In a park in Budapest.

Some passers-by
Did just that with a glance. The German fat guy
Shrugged and went his way. An escort-girl
Alone came up and stooped and touched and didn't
Go for a short while.

It was 2 pm.
Nothing happened. 'The police are going to come,
And we've no papers,' I fretted. Patrick said,
'They won't ask anything,' and an ambulance
Came and no one did.

They hauled him up.
His anorak hood fell back. Our little group
Saw now he was a girl. She could have died
Of drugs or cold, stabwound or rope or rape.
Least bad was suicide.

They drove away.
We'll never know a thing. We spent the day
In the tight conspiracy of private shocks.
A clerk in police HQ would make some notes
And slide them in a box.

A year and a half
And I'd do this, predictably enough.
In Hungary perhaps they shed some light
On why she died, but light shed on a death
Is not what I call light.

I was waiting.
To bring some writer's thinking to the writing.
Of what it was to chance on the fresh dead
In public in broad daylight in the middle
Of where we are. Instead

It's ended up as dry as a lucky stone,
Something to carry around and feel. Move on.

THE SARAJEVO ZOO

Men had used up their hands, men had
offered, cupped, or kissed them to survive,
had wiped them on the skirts of their own town,
as different men had shinned up a ladder and taken
          the sun down.

One man had upped his arms in a victory U
to a thousand others, to show how much of the past
he did not know and would not know when he died.
Another's joke was the last a hostage heard
          oh I lied

which did win some applause from the bare hands
of dozing men. And others of course had never
fired before, then fired, for the work of hands
was wild and sudden in those days
          in those lands.

For men. For the women there was
the stroke, the ripping of hair, the smearing of tears,
snot, and there was the prod of a shaking man,
or with fused palms the gibbering prayer
          to the U.N.

The nothing they had between those palms was
hope and the yard between surrendering palms
was hope as well. Far off, a fist in the sky
was meaning hope but if you prised it open
        you saw why.

The hands of the children here were wringing themselves
hot with the plight of animals over there,
and drawing them in their pens with the crimson rain
of what men do to each other on television
        crayoned in.

But hands continued to feed the demented bear
who ate two other bears to become the last
bear in the Sarajevo Zoo. And they fed him
when they could, two Bosnian zookeepers
        all autumn.

Today I read that that time ended too,
when fifteen rifles occupying some thirty
hands got there and crept in a rank on knees
towards the smoke of the blown and stinking cages
        and black trees.

Trees were what you could not see the starving
beasts behind, or see there were now no beasts,
only the keepers crouching with their two lives.
Then winter howled a command and the sorry branches
        shed their leaves.

As blank as scripture to a ruling class
Discussed in hells they do not think exist,
Cracked and abandoned to the slicing grass
      And disabusing dust,
A movie screen shows nothing in a morning mist.

Here's where the happy endings were never had,
Or, like the long and lonely, never shown.
No one rode to the rescue of who was good,
      No star was born, none shone,
No dream came true, or fun began, or life went on.

Classical outside. Like a Parthenon
Or meant to be, but more as if that mother
Had quite disowned this worn and woebegone
      Shell of light. Its father
Was a woman's face in a glass. She ordered it like weather.

Here's where the stepping leg of a pale princess
Would never gleam in the flank of a silver Merc,
No carpet lap at the tips of an angel's dress
      As that began its catwalk,
No head be turned or heart won, none have all the luck.

It had to open faster than today.
She scratched a deadline on the skin of earth.
They couldn't meet it but they couldn't say.
        They swallowed back their breath.
The sun abruptly set in each unchewing mouth.

Here's where the plans were laid, and here ignored,
Here they were changed, here lied about, here lost,
Here's where they pulled the trick they could afford,
        Here's where they paid the cost,
Where a workman sang all day, baked in a wall to the waist,

When every shortcut snapped on the one night,
Caving and bulging floors like a bigger child
Had waded from the future for a fight,
        And each thing was spilled,
Each dimly praying gap of air was found and filled.

The light went out on no one knows how few:
Interred, incinerated, a foot stuck out
Live from a ceiling waving in a shoe
        As the auditorium set,
And the sun was down, the building up, the deadline met,

And no one goes there now except to nod.
At what you get when men take on the sun.
At what men do when told to by a god
        Who's gone, and wasn't one.
How riches look in daylight when there *are* none.

THE SIGHTSEERS

We sing, we lucky pirates, as we sail,
Overladen with our creaking cargo
Of eights and nines, and imagine chains of island
Zeroes up ahead. Some of us are ill, though,
And yelp and gibber of a rushing edge,
A foam of stars, the boatswain upside down
Who grins *You told me so.*

                          We draw to the rail,
Sleepless, and we wait and, sure enough,

Behind us like our chat against the breezes,
They stir and mutter, whom we call the Sightseers,
Who stay the length of a hundred of my heartbeats.
It passes quickly with them right behind us.

I count the beats, it's how I'm brave enough
Not to cry out or vault the rail for terror—
I number them as years of my dim hundred
Soon to be gone: so I have them born to sunlight,
Burgeoning in that apple England, picked
Or fallen, then I think of them as upright,
Ideas and expectations trailing off
Across the years, and then I see them cold,
Unshockable and tired. And by the time I

Stumble in on the sixty-second heartbeat
Their eyes are red with secrets, and their heads
Are white with what has gone through an honest mind.
And then they don't believe what they are seeing.
And then they are seeing nothing, and I believe

They walk on deck because they wake and sniff
Some empty space at every century's end,
Like breath gone out, or the air of the first flowers
That ever filled their eyes, as if it's starting—
They jolt from bed and hurry from their cabins

To see strange figures clutching at a rail.
We sing, we lucky pirates, as we sail.

Fragments of an Investigative Documentary

I: CINE

Cine, sliver of history. A few minutes
finish you off in a blare of white, and the scutter
and scutter and sigh, then the lamp on and the smiling
that something, at least, is over.

Cine, chopper of Time, mercurial
slitter, century shadowing through our light:
London's sepia scuttle, a toadstool whitens
Nevada. Colour—Zapruder.

Cine. A reel was found in a vault in a place
I happened on in the course of a search. This reel
was not—but is now—the object of that search
so it's over. Which is how

poetry works, by the way. Like cine film
it yields to the bright. Like cine film it is either
print or nothing, like cine film that nothing
is sky. Like cine film

it's made of people who run towards you and cry.

Film me in silhouette. I insist. I'm not
Them prancing nags. Is that thing rolling? No?
Good. It better not be. What you got,
Rothmans? Gimme. What do you want to know?

The boy. The boy in the chariot? Oh no.
Some things I crack about, some things I don't.
You learn the worst is never long ago.
We horses live our lives in the word *won't*

But you won't understand, you undergods.
Gimme the Bushmills. Woh that hit the spot.
The boy in the chariot. Hell. It makes no odds.
It happened. Why? This isn't lit. Why not?

What was the story . . . somebody made him think
His father wasn't his father? Right, so he snaps
And goes and gets his way. Dies in the drink.
Talking of which . . . No, you pedalling chaps

Think you're as free as air though you're made of earth.
You got to obey your whims like a whipped horse
Flies. That boy. He thought about his birth.
He wanted it again. He ran his course.

How did you find me here?
      This is my refuge from all human voices,
      Their differences that shrivel into hisses
All indistinct, their faces
      Merged to the infinite grains of a far shore

Licked by the dog sea.
      Here on my noiseless meadow I ride alone,
      Ride, ride myself with the wind on my spine
While the fuelled and roaring Sun
      Mislays my name in the mess of his tyranny.

Talk to the others, friend.
      Find the unkempt Pyrois; Aethon, vain
      And cosseted by Man; then look for Phlegon
Anywhere the thin
      Are all there is, and the wind is a hurled sand.

That's his gesture. Mine?
      Mine's this solitude. I've a world to tell
      But not this world. We switched your sky into Hell
And all for a human will,
      Its pride, its point, its prick. It will come again.

How did I know it was him?
> When we were torn through clouds and the East wind
> I felt no weight on my back, heard no command,
And felt no pull, no hand,
> No pilot. No escape now. Kingdom come.

Three images, that's all.
> One was his face, the boy, his face when he lost
> The reins and then his footing—that was the last
We saw of him—he must
> Presumably have gone in a fireball—

Another was how the Moon,
> Seeing us hurtle by, reminded us all
> Of the face of a mother beside a carousel,
Worrying herself ill
> As her children wave, are gone, are back too soon

And another was afterwards.
> I lay for a good forever somewhere in the woods.
> The petrified seconds prayed, the hours wore hoods.
'You gods,' I said, 'You gods.'
> And those, I trusted, those were my final words

To men. Instead, these are . . .
> Forget Eous, leave me alone in my meadow,
> Riding myself, racing my sisterly shadow
Into the shade, where sorrow
> Wraps her and deserts me, drenched, here.

One minute, love.
You're looking at
The winner of
The 2.15,
3.38,
And 5 o'clock.
I haven't time.
I race, I work.

Ask what you want
But ask it fast.
The time you spend
Is time I lose,
Is time we've lost.
Aethon never
Loses, friend,
You got that? Ever.

The chariot?
The idiot boy?
I don't admit
And never shall
I lost that day.
He may have done.
He burned. So what?
His father's son.

The countries burned,
The oceans steamed,
The stinking wind
It filled my eyes.
I never dreamed
Years afterwards
I'd humble all
These thoroughbreds

Day in day out,
Year after year,
Beyond all doubt
Beyond compare,
The sight they fear,
Aethon, pride
Of any course
You humans ride.

If all the gold
That lights this room
Was melted, rolled
And stretched for me,
I should in time
Reach Heaven's gate
And there I'd not
Be made to wait

But rode by servants
Back to where

I rode the Heavens
Once, the Sun
Would part the air
For Aethon,
Fanfared, forgiven,
Aethon.

VIII: A SCIENTIST EXPLAINS

Would he have suffered? That depends what you mean.
Would he have suffered? Lady, let me explain.

The fire went north.
The northern Plough,
Too hot to bear it,
Plunged below
The sea; the Snake,
Sluggish and cold,
Was scorched to fury;
Boötes, old
And slow, he too
Was stricken down,
He too was dragged or stricken down
When Phaeton flew.

Would he have suffered? Suffering's hard to define.
Would he have suffered? Lady, let me explain.

He was afraid
Of heights and now
The world he knew
Was spread below
And churning. West
He'd never make,
The wounded East
Bled in his wake.
He didn't know
The horses' names,
He'd never thought to ask their names
And didn't now.

Would he have suffered? Would he have suffered pain?
Would he have suffered? Lady, let me explain.

He bore the worst
Of Heaven, curved
With poison, Scorpio!
Wild, he swerved
And lost the reins
And lost the flight.
The chariot set
This world alight:
The woods and streams,
The crops and towns,
The nations perished in their towns
As in their dreams.

Would he have suffered? That depends what you mean.
Would he have suffered? Lady, let me explain.

> Athos, Taurus,
> Helicon,
> Parnassus, Cynthus,
> Babylon,
> Ossa, Pindus,
> Caucasus,
> Olympus, Libya,
> Ismarus,
> Rhine and Rhone
> And Nile and Tiber,
> Nile and even promised Tiber?
> Steam on stone.

Would he have suffered? Suffering's hard to define.
Would he have suffered? Lady, let me explain.

> The seas had shrunk
> And all was sand,
> They felt the scorch
> In Netherland:
> Nereus sweltered,
> Neptune swore,
> The Earth appealed
> High Jupiter:
> 'I may deserve

This doom, but spare
Your Heaven itself from fire, spare
What's left to save!'

Would he have suffered? Would he have suffered pain?
Would he have suffered? Lady, let me explain.

Obviously
One shot alone,
One thunderball
From Heaven's throne,
Divided boy
From flaming car,
Made fire of him
And falling star,
A star of him
That plunged and died
In the River Eridanus, died
Far far from home.

Would he have suffered? That depends what you mean.
Would he have suffered? Lady, let me explain.

Lady?

IX: CLYMENE'S CODA

Death was instantaneous.
Death is always instantaneous.
Loss was instantaneous.
Loss is always.

X: THE HORSES' MOUTHS: PHLEGON

Get on my back. You all do in the end.
You've come some way to go the way you came,
  But shall do, all the same,
  My doubly hopping friend,
At least you ride in peace, at least you ask my name.

Where are the other three? There's no surprise.
Eous rippling aimlessly alone,
  Pyrois wrecked, Aethon?
  Neighing at blue skies,
As if his loss, our loss, was some grand race he'd won.

I work this zone. Don't have to, but I do.
I do have to, and so would you. Look now,
  The planters on the brow,
  They falter, wondering who
Wants what of them and why. They'll try to question you.

Be plain with them. It waters you with hope
That in this desert where the fire can't die
       Nor air reach to the sky,
       Somehow they grow a crop
That doesn't care it's dead, that doesn't know. Now stop,

Get off my back. Feel hotness on each sole
And howl. For this is not the word made flesh,
       This is the word made ash,
       This is the mouth made hole,
Here where the star fell, here where he got his wish.

THE WISH

Alone in spoiling it, I said I wish
That I can wish for everything. They said
That's cheating. You've one wish. I said that *is*
One wish. We sat against the paper shed.

Now, they had wished for peace on earth, for painted
Chocolate cities, flights to anywhere,
And one strange one to go with *her*—he pointed
To where she did her handstands on her hair,

Her pout flipped to a smile, as if the sky
Would grant what it amused itself to grant.
They pondered, troubled, hot with how and why,
Considering my case. When the bell went

Against my wish and that most amazing field
Began to be abandoned, as that girl
Was falling to her feet, and chocolate filled
The hands and crumbled happily, I was still

Wondering, as I was all afternoon,
If they would grant my wish. When at last they would,
I found myself at my own gate, alone,
Unwishing, backwards, everything I could.

SOMEONE AT THE DOOR

Men call it a war.
     But all it ever is for us is
Someone at the door.

What men call this affair
     Across the land alights on us as
Howling on a stair.

What men call duty-bound
     Is teenage girls and tiny children
Blinking by a mound.

What men call civil strife
     Is strangers in the weeds and a wan
Bride with a fruit-knife.

For men call it a war
     But all it ever is for us is
Someone at the door.

The cry a man can hear
     Is cut with skill upon a stone
Some forty yards from here.

The flag a man can wave
     Will go nine times around whatever's
Spooned into a grave.

And when a cannon booms
        It starts the clocks that tick forever
In our living rooms.

For men call it a war.
        But all it ever is for us is
Someone at the door.

They burned the bright estate.
        I know because I knelt and saw it
Smoulder in my grate.

Dear villages are theirs.
        And eyes of the evicted women
Dab upon my chairs.

And, marching through the mist,
        One with one door left to knock on
Starts to make a fist.

For men call it a war.
        But all it ever is for us is
Someone at the door.

A LOW GOD ON KRAFLA

A god will prick the bellies of the clouds
To see what happens; one will set the fire
To melt the place, he *knows* that happens, one
Will make a fool of blood near where we come from,
But one will make a beeline for Krafla.

Rip bits off and smell them, put them back.
Look it's easy. Crock bits off, they're rotten.
Crumble them, how struck they are, how broken.
How young and old the earth got at Krafla.
Make a wish on smoke, nobody does that.

This is really ugly. You waltz up
And note it has a kind of grandeur. Look
That's frankly puffin shit. This thing is Krafla.
This soil has never seen us and it's screaming.
Refugee would be the least crap image.

Whatever unreported war threw up this,
Here it is, terranean on Krafla:
Black, fuming, cracking, photogenic, shitey
Grey souvenir for iffy middle children.
Pocket it, think better of it, bin it.

The lowest god you get is king of Krafla.
Turn yellow at his stink. He won't show you
His fabulous lagoons so near at hand, though,
And green as heaven. Them you have to look for.
He's not as proud of what was no trouble.

THE BREAKAGE

Someone broke our beautiful
            All-coloured window. They were saints
He broke, or she or it broke. They were
            Colours you can't get now.

Nothing else was touched. Only our
            Treasured decoration, while it
Blackened in its calm last night, light
            Dead in it, like He is.

Now needles of all length and angle
            Jab at air. They frame a scene
Of frosty meadows, all our townsmen
            Bobbing here to mourn this,

To moan and wonder what would mount
            And ride so far to grieve us,
Yet do no more than wink and trash,
            Not climb down in here even.

Most eyes are on the woods, though,
            Minds on some known figures,
At least until they too turn up here,
            Sleep-white, without stories.

Things it could have done in here
            It hasn't done. It left it all
The way it was, in darkness first, now
            This, the dull light day has.

We kneel and start. And blood comes
            Like luck to the blue fingers
Of children thinking they can help,
            Quick as I can warn them.

HURRY MY WAY

After the accident of rain all night,
The doctor's fingers tapping on the body:
That window first, then this and twice at that
For anything, but I until I'm ready
Am hiding in the folds of a wet Friday.
So I won't hurry your way. Hurry my way.

When work was handed out at morning break
In the watery warm school you also went to,
I drew the blank and blushed and had to make
The best of every silence I was sent to,
Trying to figure out a reason why they
Would always hurry their way. Hurry my way.

For thirty thousand noons is how it strings
Together, this, it's really what you're roped to.
The rest is folding and unfolding things
You see, and free an arm to make a note to
See more of, but it's you against the tide. A
Wave is coming your way. Hurry my way.

And love was somewhere in the subterfuge
That suits it, but it had to come and get me.
The crowded room it glanced across was huge
And snow was falling by the time it met me.
It must have travelled each and every byway,
And that's what it calls hurry. Hurry my way.

Dark. I've not gone anywhere on this
Subterranean day, but if you'd seen it
You wouldn't have done either. Happiness
Deters me from an ending, which may mean it
May have to make things harder soon. So I say
Whack on your winter coat and hurry my way.

RIO NEGRO

FOR GERALDINE

As a boy awake in bed with a mum's kiss
He wipes can clearly see the wedge of light
He needs will thin away from him, the darkness
Falls on the uncomprehending. Night

Swallows this observation, and this male,
Curled and sailing farther than it felt
Possible away from what felt whole,
Is stretching for a handhold on the world.

The Rio Negro, nothing for a view,
Its banks in blackness like whatever things
Nor and Neither are referring to,
Bats my breath away with its slow wings.

Too weak to say I miss you, I've about
The scope of what I started with, the sliver
Of matter immaterial without
What plumps for it in just so dark a river.

I'm glad you saw me. Now you'd see me shift
Gingerly to stern to watch a sky
Stubbed by that hot city that we left
Ten hours ago. I'm glad you caught my eye.

Macaws I saw stay in the mind. They soared
And tilted in the least of the old light,
Over the treetops. If you see this bird
A captive, it's been scissored from the mate

It would have flown beside for sixty years.
My cabin-window's black as the reply
Of rivers to the I and its ideas,
Eroding them to barely one, but I

At least am moving, like the Rio Negro,
Somewhere coming helplessly to light,
And even nothing, signing itself zero,
Is paying homage like a satellite.

FOR MY DAUGHTER

If I call this poem that, I have as new
A pattern of three words to learn as you
Have everything. The day you get the gist
Of what this is becoming you'll have missed
The point you were. Then you'll have reached the stage
You stay at, insofar as every age
In writing is a step along a shelf
Where words are stowed and weather like a self.
The height is dizzy but it stays the same
And the ladder gets there when you make a name
Of something I keep calling you. That date
We won't forget, are bound to celebrate,
Like rain we needed after a long spell
Of what was blissful but incredible.

UNDER THESE LIGHTS

IN MEMORY OF JOSEPH BRODSKY

You who had dared me out under these lights
Have left them alone I see now my eyes accustom.

Gone, though your voice is hung in the heights of the ballroom,
A flex of vowels slung on a crown of hooks.

You don't have to love us now, and the leaves of books
Are flicking aloud on the lens of the first reader

To hear you from the future. I remember
That was the sound I heard, though you who made it

Were working a joke in then, like you'd decided
We knew you were only passing, weren't local,

Were out to upset us somehow. That was that chuckle:
Something to do with oxygen, fair pain,

Oasis reached at last, though knowing each sign
One could survive was not a sign for home.

EDWARD WILSON

A dream of English watercolourists
all spread out on the hills: the sky is blue.
No breeze, nothing creative, not the least
exploratory dab. Then the same view

clouds and differs. Hills on the horizon
breed and open till the light has all
its colours boiling and there's only Wilson,
sketching in a blizzard, with his whole

blood-sausage fist about a charcoal point,
grasping forever things in their last form
before the whiteness. A late English saint
has only eggs to save, himself to warm,

picturing Oriana. Lost winds
tug at the sketchbook. Shaded round, the eyes
Scott has to look at till tomorrow ends
are unenquiring and as blue as skies.

Valentine's Day anywhere the boys are,
Grouped around the sack that might as well be
Kicking like a caught thing, like a prisoner,
They sort it out so rapidly, then slowly.

They lean back amazed, then not at all amazed
At tissues ringed and arrowed to them. Plainly
This pattered here from home like a dim beast
Only the English feed. It would never guess

There is no place like home, and in home's place
Are these who sit befuddled in a fosse,
Crumpling the colour white and the colour pink
Away like news of some far Allied loss

That's one too many. Now they can only think
It's rained so long the past has burst its sides
And spilled into the future in the ink
Of untold villages of untold brides.

MY GRANDFATHER AT THE POOL

IN MEMORY OF JAMES MAXWELL (1895–1980)

This photo I know best of him is him
With pals of his about to take a swim,

Forming a line with four of them, so five
All told one afternoon, about to dive:

Merseysiders, grinning and wire-thin,
Still balanced, not too late to not go in,

Or feint to but then teeter on a whim.
The only one who turned away is him,

About to live the trenches and survive,
Alone, as luck would have it, of the five.

Four gazing at us evenly, one not.
Another pal decided on this shot,

Looked down into the box and said *I say*
And only James looked up and then away.

I narrow my own eyes until they blur.
In a blue sneeze of a cornfield near Flers

In 1969, he said *Near here*

It happened and he didn't say it twice.
It's summer and the pool will be like ice.

Five pals in Liverpool about to swim.
The only one who looks away is him.

The other four look steadily across
The water and the joke they share to us.

Wholly and coldly gone, they meet our eyes
Like stars the eye is told are there and tries

To see—all pity flashes back from there,
Till I too am the unnamed unaware

And things are stacked ahead of me so vast
I sun myself in shadows they cast:

Things I dreamed but never dreamed were there,
But are, and may be now be everywhere,

When you're what turns the page and looks away.
When I'm what disappears into my day.

LETTERS TO EDWARD THOMAS

FOR DEREK WALCOTT

I

Dear Edward, just a note to say we're here
And nowhere could be better. And your key
Was where you said it would be, and the air
Is fresh with things you think, while looking kindly
On us intruders. Jenny says let's wait,
You can't be far away, while George of course
Has toppled into every single seat
To find his favourite. Five-to-one it's yours
He'll plump for, but Team Captain of the Cottage
Declares it's not allowed. I've said we're off
On a foraging expedition to the village
And that's where we are now, or soon enough
We shall be. We can't wait to see you, Edward.
We feel as if we have. I mean your home
Was breathing softly when we all invaded.
Not only air but breath, as in the poem
       I treasure that you showed me,
Which clings and flutters in me like a leaf
And falls when I remember how you told me
You couldn't write a poem to save your life!
       Consider that thing done.
Here's just a note to say we've been and gone.

Dear Edward, just a note to say your wood
Has summoned us away, as you yourself
Hinted it might. The horde has swooped and fed
And drunk (in George's case three times) your health,
And Rose and Peter wouldn't hear of sleep,
Said it was banished back to Hampstead, swore
No path would go untrodden, and no sheep
Untroubled by us—George said: 'And no door
Of any inns unswung!' and so we're gone
A second time, though you'll have no idea
I wrote a first time. Blame the evening sun
For luring us back out. We love it here
And only you are missing. What that does
Is make us lonely. True, for all my chatter.
A beauty-spot will do that. What it has
Is one thing missing. Ask me what's the matter
         Anywhere it's beautiful
And there's your answer. Long before it's dark
You'll hear us creatures rolling up the hill
In twos, to be the last into your Ark,
         Or to be told by you
What things we missed, went by, lost, didn't do.

Dear Edward, just a note to say today
The sun came up and scooped them up like eggs,
Our hearts, and set them fourteen miles away
And said now get there on your London legs—
So off we've gone, obedient, though sure
It's nothing but an agency of you,
And so I pin this to the master's door
In sure and certain hope you'll be there too,
With all our hearts at journey's end, in some
Vale of picnic-cloth. Last night we played
The word-games Adam taught to Eve, and some
Eve knew but never told him. Jenny made
A game of 'Where was Edward?' which I won
By saying you were walking and had paused
To hear two nightingales—and not gone on
Until you'd taught them singing. This had caused
       The rumpus of all time
Amid the birds, which we could hear from here,
One saying, 'Do we teach him how to rhyme?'
And all the rest as far as Gloucestershire
       Going, 'Yes, don't you remember?'
George said you'd walked so far it was November.

4

Dear Mr Thomas, now it's been so long
We lost your first name in the meadow grass
At dusk, when on a road we thought was wrong
We started recognising things. Your house
Then viewed us dimly. But you must excuse
The new meander in my messages,
And blame it on the elderflower juice
That George said would be *choice* with sandwiches
And seems so to have been. We all agree
We shall not leave tomorrow if our host
Insists on his invisibility,
And clears the table round us like a ghost
And seems to comment in the silences.
Rose and Peter have to leave, but George
Declares this week is cancelled, or his is.
Or so we can infer from how he snores.
          I tried to start some games
But after walking longer than we've ever,
Who's in the mood for folding up the names
Of ones we know in town? Who cares whose lover
          Really cares for whom?
Our heads are bowed and spinning in the room.

Dear Edward, just a note to say I left
A quiverful all weekend, in the hope
You'd sit down at your table. Here we laughed
And lolled for what seemed ages, and sat up
For what seemed scarcely time at all, but only
To see grey dawn arrive and blush to find us
Watching, late enchanted into early.
It's Monday noon and everything's behind us.
Rose and Peter took the six-fifteen,
As George and Jenny meant to. They at last
Boarded the nine o'clock, George in a dream
He started telling as the engine hissed,
Commissioning them for London. So I'm left
Abandoned to restore the place to how
It looked on that bright morning we arrived,
That seems so long ago. Time is so slow
        Without you. Then again
The moment that I shut the door, no doubt
You'll reach the gate and grin and ask me when
My friends are coming. I'll ask you about
        Your poems, as if you'd say,
Knocking the ashes from your favourite clay.

6

To punish you I threw the note away
I wrote you in your kitchen. Now my thanks
Are scribbled among strangers as we sway
Through Hampshire towards town, and the sun blinks
Behind the poplars. Edward Thomas, great
Unknowable, omniscient, your cottage
Waits for you: no sign we ever sat
Around your fire, no trace of pie or porridge,
Nor dreg of George's ale remains. No talks
Of ours will last the time you take to light
Your clay, and your first steps will make our walks
As brief and viewless as a shower at night.
These are our heartfelt thanks. We could have haunted
Many houses where we wouldn't see you.
At yours we thought it likely to be granted
Sight or sound, but it was not to be. You
       Were needed in the field,
By hawk or hedge, who knows, their need was greater
Than ours, who wanted names for things revealed
That we should know by now or may ask later.
       And reason not my need,
Who writes what nobody but she will read.

Poem to Mr Thomas and Mr Frost,
Created by a dandelion you passed
As you in talk about a stanza crossed
Half Herefordshire, till you sat at last
In silence. I'm the dandelion that saw
Two aspens shake and shed in a quick wind,
And tried to loose her own leaves to the floor
Like they did and did manage in the end,
When they were both long gone in the great storm.
One to the west and one to the east, away
Towards the blood-commander in the dawn
And all his soldiers, pink becoming grey.
And you won't see this, if you live as long
As what you sent me: 'As the team's head-brass'
It starts but isn't titled. If I'm wrong
And your great hands one day are holding these
       Dandelion hairs,
The storm would not have come, the trees have kept
Their ground, and through the hearts of all the shires
Would Mr Thomas and Mr Frost have stepped
       And war like a rough sky
Been overlooked in talk, and blown on by.

Poem for Mr Edward Eastaway,
Who lives here care of me, so no one knows
His name is Rumpelstiltskin and by day
He rips your verse to pieces in great prose.
By night he turns his prose to poetry
Because a poet told him to who saw
A mighty fine recruit for poverty
And wrote the line that opened his front door.
They have rejected Edward Eastaway
Again: the letter came this afternoon.
One knows precisely what a fool will say
Somehow. We've many stars to the one moon
In our night sky, but all that makes a face
Of that recurring rock is the one sun
It likes, without which it must find its place
To hide behind, or make believe it's gone.
      Edward Eastaway,
Whose name that isn't and whose time it ain't,
Who's living here or was just yesterday,
Or in Wales, Wiltshire, Oxfordshire or Kent,
      The rumour's that you crossed
The Channel. Stanza-break, growls Mr Frost.

Dear Father Thomas, every Christmas Eve
Good children of the world are quite as shy
As I am to write *Dear* and then believe
For twenty lines our goodness could be why
It's worth our time. Our faith turns to this thread
That shuttles downward while the mischievous
Need nothing but a coal-sack by the bed,
And wake to the same carols. Each of us
Is writing, Edward, asking the great space
Below us what is missing still, what gift
Will make us whole again. We fold and place
Our answers in the chimney and are left
These pink embarrassed authors by the fire.
We all talk tommy-rot we understand.
Somebody coughs, politely to enquire
Did they not kick a ball on No Man's Land
        Two years ago? 'That's so,'
Smiles Peter, adding: 'Not tonight, I fear.'
And I hear George's voice say: 'Cricket, though,
So Edward gets a knock.' But he's not here,
        George, he's where you are,
Restless tonight like all good children are.

One dead was sent a Valentine, so both
Were spared their lover's blushes. What I write
Is on its way nowhere, is less than breath,
So might be anything, as nothing might.
It's that there's nothing now that doesn't seem
As if it's where it ended. All the paths
Beyond this word or this become the same:
Thickets, or a handing-down of deaths
As by a school official, not a teacher,
A visiting official by one gate.
Now all the hope there is is in a picture
Of P. E. Thomas gone, because my fate
Is never to foresee, believed or no.
Is to be wrong. These words are packing up
And going. Words I mean you not to know
Don't see why they should move in any step
      I fix them with. So go,
You English words, while he's alive, and blow
Through all of him so Englishmen will know
You loved him and who cares how long ago,
      And hide him from the light
He'll strike and hold until his clay's alight.

Dear Edward, when the war was over, you
Were standing where a wood had been, and though
Nothing was left for you to name or view
You waited till new trees had hidden you.
Then you came home and in a forest called
The Times your name was found, and not among
The officers but in a clearing filled
With verses, yours. Then your new name was sung
With all the old. And children leafing through,
And old men staring and their daughters stilled
With admiration: all this happened too,
Or had already by the time you pulled
The book I hide this in from your top shelf
And blew its dust away. The year is what,
1930? '80? Please yourself,
But do remember as you smile and sit
       That everything's foreseen
By a good reader, as I think I am
On David's Day of 1917,
Reaching for blotting-paper. Now's the time
       To fold this work away
And find me on this bleak or brilliant day.

Choose me, *Sie deutsche Worte*. This is the first
Of all the letters you will never read,
Edward. I was shy in my own west
Always, so you never read a word
I sent, but this is written with as clear
A mind as has been opened like a shell.
'Greatly loved in the battery,' writes this dear
Major Lushington, who says you fell
In early morning with some battle won
And all the soldiers dancing. You were loved
In the battery and in the morning sun
Brought out the blessed clay, when something moved
Like cloud perhaps. The major asked us round
To tell us you knew nothing. That your book
Of Shakespeare's sonnets that they knelt and found
Was strangely creased and the clay didn't break
       Which Helen gave your son,
And Robert's *North of Boston* in your kit
They gave to me, not needing it. And when
They reached you you were not marked, not hit,
       Breeze blowing in your hair,
Chosen. What had stopped your heart was air.

Dear Edward, now there's no one at the end
There's nothing I can't say. Some eight or nine
I have by heart. Your farmer-poet friend
Is flying around the world on a fine line
That starts in you, or grows out from the days
You passed together. England is the same,
Cheering to order, set in its new ways
It thinks are immemorial. The Somme
Has trees beside it but some shovel-work
Will bring the dead to light. There's so much more
I want to say, because the quiet is dark,
And when the writing ends I reach a shore
Beyond which it's so cold and that's what changed,
Edward, on that Easter Monday. You
Were land to me, were England unestranged,
Were what I thought it had amounted to,
       But look at the fields now,
Look eyelessly at them, like the dug men
Still nodding out of Flanders. Tell them how
You walked and how you saw, and how your pen
       Did nothing more than that,
And, when it stopped, what you were gazing at.

Dear Edward Thomas, Frost died, I was born.
I am a father and you'd like the names
We gave our girl. I'm writing this at dawn
Where Robert lived, in Amherst, and your poems
I keep by his, his house-brick to your tile.
I teach you to my students, and aloud
I wonder what you would have come to. While
I wonder they look out at a white cloud
And so we pass the time. Perhaps I'll guess
Which one will ask me what they always ask:
Whom do I write for? Anybody? Yes,
You. And I'll walk home in the great dusk
Of Massachusetts that extends away
Far west and north, the ways you meant to go
To save your life. A good end to the day,
That's going to be. It's going to be cool, though,
       I see out in the town,
And start to turn the trees to what the world
Comes flocking here to see: eight shades of brown
Men never saw, and ninety-nine of gold,
       More shades than can have names,
Or names to bring them back when the snow comes.

AND INDIANS

They made a word for light when it went out,
Then many words for dark, if not such dark
As fell and spread among them like a doubt.

It's not a date we celebrate, but then
There's no one day to ring or week to mark.
It happened and keeps happening to them.

Nothing to make a song or dance about.
Nothing to be the theme of a third act.
They had no argument and show no sign

Of coming back to make one. They were *them*,
And death is in that word like its own wine
Gone acid and eroding them to *then*.

Then to the fled allotment of a time.
Then to the listed ruin of a fact.

ON A DEVON ROAD

Whatever thoughts there were for me on a Devon road,
nothing knotted them suddenly to one spot
like what lay up ahead, flopped and brownish,
too much of it for a bird, too much for a fox;
one wound as I went by its snouted head
had trickled; the slightest movement was beyond it.

It was a badger. I looked back over my shoulder
twice at it and a third time turned, I was staring:
its stillness had a force and a beat that nothing
green remotely had. It was pulsing
with having been. It was not what was around it.
Where it and the world met was a real edge—

like someone thumping 'badger' to the page
with a finger and old Remington had banged
a hole with b clean through, and couldn't mend it,
that dumb dot in his title word, and had to
use his hand to stop light coming through it.

DAWN ON THE MIDI

In the one pink hour these villas
have to themselves before the English voices;
in the time before the couple
start winding back the eyelids of the windows,
I pass as close as one who needs to see them
can pass to the lost owners

who are riding the end carriage
of the Blue Train, to the sheet of light they'd fashioned
to flutter for a time
between them and a future that was waiting
politely by, with hands as disinclined
to mercy as a clock's are,

or smiling at the window
of the First Class then running backwards waving
saddened into smoke though—
two sights she wakes from on a lip of light
and ribbon and remembers where she is now,
mid-afternoon in heaven,

and soon to be seen stepping
the marble staircase, all the hood and fuss
with the viewfinder crucial,
while the twelve at lunch, or whist, beside the palm-tree
go quiet as now, passing as close as any
who won't see you can pass

to you who note them plainly,
or me in this bird-yellow hour these houses
have to themselves, while the breeze
has breath enough to puff the toys in races
across our idle and impulsive pool,
stone-deaf to the sea breaking.

[FROM BOOK I: THE CHANCE IN HELL]

When the train stopped I started and woke up.
Was nowhere, as before, no change in that.
Nothing new in trundling to a stop

where nothing seemed to call for one. The light
was winter afternoon, with 'afternoon'
a term for darkness. In the cold and wet

were trees beside the line, grey evergreen
unknown by name. And not a soul to hail,
I said again and with a smile so thin

it died before its life. And not a soul,
I called. The sky was murk, its memory
of sunshine like my memory of school,

of sunshine in the morning. Next to me
my hands were inching off the dirty felt
towards each other, meeting gingerly,

lovers twining, brothers known and held,
then strangers upright like the poor in prayer.
My eyelids met in secret, my eyes filled

with vision, then reopened on nowhere.
I craned against the glass to see ahead
and did see lights along the way so far,

but into nothing known, and I sat forward,
hands set on my knees, and, weighed down
with swallowing, I scanned them. What I said

when I was ready I had voiced alone
so many times. I said: 'This is the day
of freedom. If the day will prove me wrong,

the day will never come and I'm away
forever.' This I said, these were the words
I had. I said my name was Edmund Lea,

to stitch a little wing on my few words
so they could fly. Then I was on my feet,
glancing out again at the rainy woods

and the rain beyond the window scribbling it.
I made my way to the men's. An hour had come
I'd waited for like an island for a boat

that never comes, like a boatman for a home
he doesn't have, and where did I have to be?
—I giggled as I wiped—in the white room.

'The day will never come and I'm away,'
I called into the flush, 'for all of Time.
I hope I'm home. My name is Edmund Lea,

I stand before you every day the same,
I stand before the emptiness, I lean,
I kneel to it, I beg to be brought home.'

I curled into a fold of prayer, my frame
I curled into that type of form. The lights
came on along the carriage one by one

as if to bid me to regain my wits,
and I rose and shuffled back in a dull shame
at my poor prayer towards the numbered seats.

And there he was, there's where I found *him*,
slouched across two places, a young man
and fast asleep or so it—oddly—seemed,

so suddenly he'd come. I hadn't seen,
I calculated, any soul at all
in sixteen days, since from the slowing train

I saw one man with buckets by a well.
No one I ever saw again, and no one
ever on this train. It was not Hell

you know about. No one seen again,
no one in here, and no one speaking this,
the English language. This was not a tongue

they spoke in Hell. Theirs was a gibberish
devoid of rhyme or reason. But this one,
perhaps a student, in his early twenties,

appeared here when we stopped a while in rain.
And his empty book fell open as he snored,
and the pages leafed themselves until they came

decisively to a page that bore the word
Poems, bore the English word for poems,
Poems, and I weakened then and cried.

I didn't even wake him with these moans
of bliss. They were the train, perhaps he thought,
grilling itself for stopping here. My hands

were shuddering to the page to be a part
of English, of these *Poems*, though I could see
he'd written nothing in it, or not yet—

the devils in me told me in my glee,
Blow me, it's all coincidence and Poems
means in his world 'Help!' or 'Edmund Lea,

I've come to nail a lid on all your dreams
of seeing home again!' And then my fingers
reached the page and stuck there like names.

This woke him, and his book fell down between us.

[FROM BOOK 3: MY FIRST POEM]

In recollection what descended then,
that cold illuminated mist, remained
till Christmas, made a candle of each friend

emerging, disappearing in it, made
each smile a call to shelter; but in truth
it must have lifted on forgotten days

and let them by. What's kept of it is breath,
that's certain, fog-white utterance of gossip
overhead, a trade in rumour, myth,

complicity. The girls around the steps
at Record Time, Nick Straton sauntering by
in his hairy hooded coat, the talk of trips

gone bad in London, freakouts in the country,
nights of ill-lit deep emotional candour,
in blankets then, the sunrise ceremony,

drowsing. Christmas Eve in the town centre,
there they are—I see them clear as type—
Stan, Mendis, Russ, Nick Straton, and some other

name that's gone. They're slouched along a step
below the Great War monument; their breath
is white with cold or brown with smoke. 'Slide up,'

Stan calls. 'I'm Christmas shopping.' 'Catch your death?'
says Nick, thudding a fag from his gold pack
to point at me. I join them. 'Hanging with?'

they're asking me. Stan says, 'We went electric,
Lea, we got a session round at Nick's.
You hanging with?' I smoke, the little frantic

sucks we used to take. 'Lay down some tracks,'
they're telling me. The Hunger was their band,
they started it one term, they played some gigs

at parties, we stirred drinks and stood around,
amazed at them for looking that like stars,
just standing there. They made a muddy sound

and no one danced. We saw their bright guitars,
their skilful hands, their amplifiers and cords,
the nonchalance, the chance . . . There are no chairs

in Nick's garage, it's dark, they crowd towards
the back for a band meeting. I'm alone;
I glide my hand along the chill bronze threads

of an idle bass guitar. The boy called Moon
rides up, he's excellent. Nick doesn't play,
he sings their songs, he sings in a low drone

I can't decipher. Now the band is ready,
counting four and starting, such a noise—
I sit on a sagging box and wonder only

when on earth I can buy presents now, in these
last hours of Christmas Eve. A light goes on
in mid-song, in mid-song, that memory

I swear by, all six of them—Stan, Moon,
Nick, Russ, Dodge Mendis and the drummer—each
in some way falters. Nick says through the song,

down the loud blasting microphone, 'The switch,
the switch!' Out goes the light again, and I,
I think he's called the girl who's come *this witch*,

this witch to break their spell? And I'm wondering why
and who it is until it is Clare Kendall
who stands there listening, so improbably,

Clare, who halts there, tinted by the purple
bulb they use for light, in her long coat,
Clare, who yawns and makes the cutting signal

past her throat. Nick Straton booms out, 'What?'
at which she rolls her eyes, and since the track
is not about to finish, turns her head

and stretches through between Stan Burke and Nick
to where I'm watching this. I feel my side,
my right side seem to warm or somehow quicken

at how she sits quite near, and my left side,
I can recall it, seems so cold and dragged
I pity it. The Hunger play so loud

the noise is dreadful, but I recollect
these moments always as the purest silence . . .
Her scribble passed to me on a train ticket

suddenly in my hand: *BIRTH OF A LEGEND*.
Mine passed to her: *DEATH OF A CHRISTMAS EVE!*
Hers on a shop receipt: *LET'S SAVE THE PATIENT* . . .

The song cranks to a stop. 'It's better live,'
says Mendis as the drummer peters out,
and Nick's complaining, 'That ain't long enough,

Staz, I got another verse.' 'Nah, mate,
my solo ends it,' and they're toe to toe,
while Russ asks, 'Dig it, Lea?' and I say, 'Great,'

as Russ and Dodge are standing near us now,
dumb about the girl. 'Jimi's returned,'
she tells them, 'but we're going to have to blow.'

Nick hears this and stops arguing. 'You can't,
you got to stay.' 'I *gotta wot*?' she wonders,
Dodge Mendis says, 'The next track's called "Burned",

it's about some crazy chick.' 'Oh really, Mendis,'
Stan's now saying. 'Anyone we know?'
Nick storms out. Through the small garage window

I see him looking back, and I know now
he really liked her, but it's me she takes
back into town at dusk, it's me somehow.

[FROM BOOK 5: MALLAREA]

At times there's little mystery to how
I felt, it takes you little to get there.
And should you want to, you can set out now,

take map and money and go anywhere
you never went in England, where a mall
spreads from the railway line. Should you want to share

further, only stand in that high hall,
look upward, be the only one to, stare
out the grey skylights, be the only still

contemplative creation to be there,
then say, with force and clarity, bright tones
to bring detectives running: *I am where*

I used to live. These people are my friends.
This was my only home . . . This simple game
may help you picture me. Picture my hands

grasping the other shoulder to be warm,
my feet unsteady in a world at last
of many and on ground that stays the same;

picture me peering at it, see me pushed
past by accident, me chuckled at
for my old coat, observe me spun to rest

on a sun-yellow bench where Polly sat.
They'd lost me or I'd lost them in the crowd
around a band of drummers. There the beat

had got me swaying and I sang aloud
whatever words came by. Then when I looked
they'd gone. At least I'd found her. 'I'm afraid,'

she said while doing lipstick, 'that, in fact,
you're really lost up here.' What *up here* meant
I couldn't tell. 'If you was all an act,

if you was all an act or if you weren't,
eachways it's just as lost. I hate this place,
I done my shopping, Saturday I done it,

only time I could. It's just for Woz
I thought I'd come here so he gets his done.
Get the last train to Dad's.' She lined her eyes

with a violet crayon: 'Know what this is? *Poison*.'

[FROM BOOK 7: DEMUNDO]

. . . They are assembled in the room
to film themselves and film me go away

into the place I go. I look for him,
Wasgood, my old friend, and see he's there,
grinning at me with the welcome grin

of one oblivious, and I seem to care,
as I remember. I see all the girls
about the place, and it perfects the air

to see them smile. I envy the four walls
that each will see them when no curtain here
can hold the sky back from its meal of colours,

and I can feel my enemy, his copper
ice in my own pocket, the sour coins
he deals to me, the red-eye, the decliner.

That all around me is a site of bones
is not worth writing: writing will itself
defy it, fleshing out its broken lines

for all it's worth. They formed a ring, the twelve,
when I was close to sleep. I heard the rain's
sublime disinterest starting to dissolve

whatever would remain. I saw my hands
begin to rise, ten fingers outward, those
and these still seeing eyes, somehow to send

a word to the sad twelve—to shield my eyes
was all I thought my hands and eyes could do.
But that was wrong—I'd have friends recognise

the sight of them was dear; besides, no view
could frighten me. I made my hands embrace
in prayer and glanced above—*I can't see you,*

I whispered so that no one heard—and last
my palms were upward-facing and my sight
was on each person till each realised.

And then my eyelids, with inhuman might,
began to roll the screens across. I heard
the hum of filming and a voice too sweet

to keep me conscious—*Angel, say a word*—
then I was waking, and my face could feel
a rash of air, iron smell, and I beheld

a flock of birds fly up and turn, then wheel,
dark on the sky, white on a passing field.

PLAYGROUND SONG

When over the playground once they came
        to tag me It then dance away,
I danced away and to my shame
        they're waiting for me to this day.

When I was called to answer why
        I wasn't there, I wasn't there.
All afternoon you hear them cry
        explain this at an empty chair.

When Juliet confided whom
        she loved and would I let him know,
light-heartedly I left the room,
        forgot it till an hour ago.

And tiny things too late to do
        have gone so far they can't be seen
except at dusk by me and you,
        and though I hide till Halloween

you never come, not even now
        each hand has reached the other sleeve,
not even now the light is low
        and green as you would not believe.

THE SEA COMES IN LIKE

NOTHING BUT THE SEA

The sea comes in like nothing but the sea,
but still a mind, knowing how seldom words

augment, re-orders them before the breaker
and plays them as it comes. All that should sound

is water reaching into the rough space
the mind has cleared. The clearing of that mind

is nothing to the sea. The means whereby
the goats were chosen nothing to the god,

who asked only a breathing life of us,
to prove we were still there when it was doubted.

THE NERVE

Somewhere at the side of the rough shape
your life makes in your town,
      you cross a line,
      perhaps

in a dusty shop you pause in, or a bar
you never tried, and a smell
      will do as well;
      then you're

suddenly very far from what you know.
You found it as a child,
      when the next field
      to you

was the world's end, a breeze of being gone.
Now it begins to give,
      a single nerve,
      low down:

it sags, as if it felt the gravity
at long last. You are chilled
      to have been told
      that way—

but you ought to recognise it, it's the one
that may well fail one day,
   fail utterly,
   go wrong,

be Judas, while the others, without thought
of you, or of your pain,
   show no sign,
   are mute,

assume they're safe with you. Treasure the nerve
suggesting otherwise;
   treasure its dis-
   belief:

it's straining to see the outline of somewhere
inhospitable,
   with other rules,
   unfair,

and arbitrary, something to endure,
which nonetheless you spot,
   contemplate,
   start for;

where you will face the choices that the nerve
has suffered: to be plucked
   and, for that act
   of love,

to have brought the soldiers running; to lie low,
and, for that act of fear,

      have perished years

      ago.

GATEKEEPERS ON DANA

The first act
of the first light in the east
is to make gatekeepers of those great twin pines
on Dana Street:

to find them,
the needs and fissures in them,
make heralds of them, the first of all to affirm
by their aspect

the emergency,
or chillingly to imply
the amplitude of what's to come. When it's gone,
what it is,

and you wonder
what cranks the shadows round
together like the beasts at a long feeding,
who, finishing,

move off,
don't try to ask that pair,
because if you do they will ask themselves *what gate
has he in mind,*

then brush and murmur,
why would it need keeping?
shiver and hazard: *Are you expecting something?*
Tell all.

THE LEONIDS

The corners of our eyes,
cold and alert to missing them, report
a flash, and in the breeze
      we turn our heads
to where the stars are quiet.

It goes against the grain,
to understand what's next is going to shoot
from anywhere. The brain,
      seeing a thing
so like itself, falls flat.

Leonids. A word,
as if they had some source or destiny,
as if this utmost speed
      they hurtle at
were theirs—towards, away—

and not our burning loop
that lights the dust they are. As if this date
were something that they keep,
      appointment reached
neither too soon nor late,

but punctual to the end.
Leonids. *Our word, our speed, our date,*
bawls the affronted mind,
          shaking the fixed
stars this way and that.

HAUNTED HAYRIDE

At the near edge of the field, a dollar a shot,
the haycart waited with its horse and man,
handing the children on and their mothers on,
unhanding them to a place on a haycart seat,

swivelling for the next. The field was a farm
beginning by Route 9, a mile at most
from town and our life here. It seemed to us
it was all farm to the start of the next farm.

It was selling its things to everyone whose plans
had ground to a stop on the road that afternoon.
Round here if you stop long enough then *boom*—
tall women come in cardigans and jeans

and everything's a stall. Car-passengers,
grey and fit and buckled in there, lifers,
all turned back to their sentences, but whatever
opens unexpectedly to strangers

possessed us, so we slowed, and stopped. The haycart
was both the farthest and the first of things
we saw, beyond the gift-shop selling pumpkins
for luck, and ghosts and Indians for mascots.

So instead we ambled up towards the sign,
making an M with Alfie's arms, Maxwells,
past pumpkin heaps and jars on the haybales,
towards the horse and cart and the haycart man.

He handed the children on and the mothers on,
and cleared a space for three, till it felt to us
like the gap was suddenly waiting for us, and this
intervened. And the look on the haycart man

intervened. So did the scope of the field,
stretching away from Saturday like a hand,
out into Massachusetts, towards England,
into the past, and from it. The air filled

with cold and we chose pumpkins at a stall.
Two, and two toys for Alfie. There was a card
explaining what their dollar for the cart
would get them: it would get them a ghost tale,

some spookiness in daytime. It had rolled
by then, that wagon. I could see its pale
brown halted speck from the highway, as if hell
were littleness, and they were being told.

THE GAME ALONE

The Purple School and its sworn enemy
contend again. I sidle in among those
        seeing it: alumni of the Purple,
and opposite numbers—literally, each class
in Magic Marker: womenfolk of '70
        proffer pies in frilled tents, in an oval

round the patterned field. I stroll a lap
in coat and scarf along the generations,
        '80, '64, grey men in sportswear,
already smiling at the leading question,
and thirty autumns pass as they look up
        to hear announcements crackling from somewhere.

One mascot's like a man, one's like a bull.
The man's huge plaster head is done to look
        colonial, bewigged; he's on the side
of everyone I'm sitting with, for luck,
while they deride him over there, they howl
        and make bull horns, bent fingers to the head.

The Purple flag flies here. Both sides of course
are cheer-led by those girls and by this brute
        who stomps along the stand in a tracksuit,
bellowing at the old folks to support.
Below, the game goes on and a side scores.
        I think of asking how and decide not;

it suddenly feels like asking television,
though television knows. In fact I change,
   stroll round, become a White-on-Scarlet guy,
why not. Our chant is going up—'Revenge!'—
and a row of girls, all blonde and loyal and frozen,
   try joining in just as it dies away.

I notice, when the game is in its times
of rest (again), that this whole bank of people
   is gazing out across the churning river,
at a world where what is white is coloured purple,
but otherwise all's well. A fresh face beams
   to see its twin, souls gladden with a shiver.

From far away, from that wide field away,
the bucket-headed mascot from the past
   turns all the rest to background. It's a game,
you want to say when seeing him, when faced,
and your skull small. The stands and hills and sky
   go darker than expected in the time,

for there's a light that it can seem the game
alone is generating. A great cheer
   on mine—the bull side—and it almost ends,
with the old-timers wobbling up to roar,
vocabulary boiled down to a name,
   and it does end, when thirty-seven seconds

vanish from the screen—a voice confides,
they're running down the clock—far over there,
       the crowd leaps up, and over here it sits.
The field lets go its lines; it doesn't care
who scampers on to form the ring of weeds
       around a violet mushroom-crop of helmets,

or the off-white and muddy red melee
disintegrating to some weary boys
       bareheaded between parents. Now it's cold
and finished. Down among the beaten guys
three girls are searching. All their jerseys say
       ATHLETICS in the dusk. They find and hold

their treasures, 45, 8, 84,
and try to speak that body language, bowed
       dismay, though in a secret swirl of joy
to be the one despondent at his side.
The winners melt away and can have more.
       The losers hold the field. Too suddenly

for some, here comes the Purple flag, the guy
is taunting us—not us, I mean my side—
       by streaming it below our wooden stand,
lording it with something not quite pride,
more personal, all his. As he runs by,
       this White-on-Scarlet, talking with a friend,

shoots out a hand that gets it, jerks the cloth
half off its stick, and stops him in his track.
   I'm very near. The victor is amazed
that happened and is grinning but in shock,
his eyes wondering *What now?* They are both
    lost for an act. The third one's realised,

and, setting free the flag, averts a scene.
So the bearer wanders on, unsure, long fields
    between him and his home. No one close by
knows quite what's to be done with what he feels;
they file away in time, treading the green
    homewards, passing strangers on the way,

contemporaries from the long-rivalled school,
or their own schoolmates who were in the future.
    All things have been exchanged, and I can't see
by now who'd cheered for what. It seems much darker
than anyone could play in. A tall girl
    is carrying the bull mask by the eye,

and as I look back nothing in the stands
can stay. Things seem to drain in unison
    down the field and chuckle through the gates,
things tilted from the world. The feeling's gone;
I'm left with it. I scribble with blue hands
    and head home through a car park, by fog lights.

Everyone had to leave in a bloody hurry.
No one had to come here. Those that did—
the ones who should be sorry were not sorry.
The ones who shouldn't be

run restaurants or laundromats or serve you
shyly in the mall. Exquisite hands
show you your change. Or chattily they drive you
when you're too tired to say,

when all the diddy icons on the dashboard
tremble. It's your town and not your town
when you leave tips for them. What's barely whispered
where they meet is true:

they might encounter him from the old world,
who came at night, who giggled at their papers . . .
Might see him smoking by the baseball field,
padding towards the diner,

lip-reading in the library. That man
escaped here, he too sobbed or stared ahead,
made landfall; he eats pretzels in the line.
They are aware he's there

both when he is and isn't there. No crimes
will stick in the new life. There is no court
in session for the narratives and claims
their voices split to make,

no angles to examine. There are times
they jump and times they clasp. There is a wood
they come to in a downpour, or have dreams
they come to in a downpour.

THE FLOOD TOWNS

At the midnight of the August day appointed,
a thousand or so
          remaining inhabitants of the doomed towns
popped champagne

at the abrupt cessation of town business,
of community
          in any legal sense, the last agreement
being that spree

till two o'clock, when all at once car headlamps
lit the hillside.
          And in the morning those who had been ready
were gone,

leaving behind eight ragged families
with nowhere else
          to be, and these it would have been who heard
the very first

tinkering of rain upon the rooftops,
or saw its fingers
          spot the windows, sniffed it through the door
opened to save

the washing, and perhaps it did sound different,
the rain this time,

       not because it was fiercer, more aware
than former rain,

but because it fell for hours in the hearing
of folk who knew

       none in heaven or earth with any stake
in stopping it.

A HUNTING MAN

Nothing but snow about. A hunting man
set out from his own truck and his sleeping son,

who followed him, found no one, and was found
five days later frozen to the ground.

His father had been nothing but a fool.
He went about his chores, he went to school

for nothing, and he waited in his truck.
The days were featureless and the nights black

he drove into. He hunted in that place,
he camped there in the trees, he heard the ice

shifting in the branches. 'Not the best,'
his sister told a lady from the press,

'the thing he did,' and chatted on the path.
But he'd assured her that his Christian faith

prevented him from carrying out his will.
A judge considered thirty days in jail

appropriate for manslaughter. The man
dissented, and some yards from where his son

was found he shot himself. Nothing but snow
about, nothing but trees, nowhere to go.

Peace is as poor a word for what he has
as *Silence* is for what it signifies.

Justice softens to sweet nothings here.
Love holds its own, admit it, as before.

THE YEAR IN PICTURES

For the Year-in-Pictures feature,
that annual old favourite,
the man behind the night desk

was dealing with five thousand
possibles at high speed,
a speed at which his blond head

was shaking and his fingers
propelling off so many
the air was never empty

of the white-backed and numbered
snapshots as they fluttered
earthward in succession.

THE ONLY WORK

IN MEMORY OF AGHA SHAHID ALI

When a poet leaves to see to all that matters,
nothing has changed. In treasured places still
      he clears his head and writes.

None of his *joie-de-vivre* or books or friends
or ecstasies go with him to the piece
      he waits for and begins,

nor is he here in this. The only work
that bonds us separates us for all time.
      We feel it in a handshake,

a hug that isn't ours to end. When a verse
has done its work, it tells us there'll be one day
      nothing but the verse,

and it tells us this the way a mother might
inform her son so gently of a matter
      he goes his way delighted.

This is for him, the writer, him I term
the creature of two feet, for he'd present
his face two feet away. He made a warm
glow to see by, willing and well-meant,
but not, I'd have to say, for the long haul.
Things he began were things I'd have to end,
I sensed immediately. When I recall
the touch of what he did with his near hand

the mood comes over me, but the mood goes,
and that reminds me too. November days
the thought of him resolves into a voice
that states *it matters now*—so does the wind,
but neither moves a muscle of my face
before it dies as if it read my mind.

HIDE AND SEEK

Of all the things to win at. There I am,
Immobilised except for my young gut,
Which does its jellyfish and does its clam
Because you've come to double-check the hut:

And the relief is evangelical
That I can breathe again and show my face,
Until all other faces show that all
Are found and mine was the last hiding place.

Then many draw to it as to a shrine,
In glum approval, jealous but sincere,
That of the silences you favoured mine,
And the last thing that mattered mattered here.

THE SURNAMES

FOR MATTHEW BELL

There being no word to hand without its hole for light,
its origins, its loss as I set eyes on it,

there being nothing that had come to nothing else,
I took the recollected way to school and back.

It was a clear day, in that it felt cleared for this,
and hedges neat and hedges ragged passed me by.

The streets were lanes again, the houses cottages,
my life so far a daydream of a life ahead,

my life ahead at home in what had gone before,
my hands in pockets for a mile of afternoon.

These afternoons are gifted but are left alone
to dabble in the sun. The thing they leave to dry

is their own town in childhood and its look in age.
Each cottage brought a name and surname into mind.

Each surname brought a face and a recalled event
that made it catch my eye, hang like a coat of arms

a moment. At the pace I walked, the pace at which
they slip the mind, the surnames might instead have been

white crosses in a formal line, where proper nouns
and silence meet and all that comes of it are flowers.

A PROMISE

I made my child a promise, so a weight
was passed to her. I saw how carefully

its power was handled, that it lit the thoughts
around it, and I felt it warm her talk

and urge the hours along. Since I, like you,
no longer know a word like that, the light

she gained was lost to me. It didn't mean
I'd let her down—I didn't—but I seemed

to be aligned with those who might in time,
as if I'd somehow set coordinates.

A CHILD'S WEDDING SONG

Thumb and finger make a ring
       to see the future through.

I can see the world through it,
       only the world and you,

only the world and you alone.
       If I should break this ring,

where will I find you in the world
       though I find everything?

The bloom between blue-pink and cherry-pink
on our north wall was new, began, was out—
one of the splendours made to make us think
it's time to learn some names. We'd done without
            since coming here in winter, in the grey.

The bird with the three semi-tones, the bird
that seems to be half air, the butterfly
that seems to be half everything but word—
we sat and thought, It's time. It is our house.
            We won't, though, I know us. We like to see

stuff strain at us from nothing, through the space
alarm in kind or colour or degree,
be there, not have been there and appear now—
then yellow at the wall in the few days
            following, and fail not knowing how.

Or be the bird long gone though its song weighs
on in us, be dead, be oceanbound
for all we know. We rest on all we know,
our little bench, and watch the trees around
            in turn unsettle, like an hour ago.

THE SNOW VILLAGE

In the age of pen and paper,
when the page was a snow village,
when days the light was leafing through
descended without message,

the nib that struck from heaven
was the sight of a cottage window
lit by the only certain
sign of a life, a candle,

glimpsed by a stranger walking
at a loss through the snow village.
All that can flow can follow
that sighting, though no image,

no face appear—not even
the hand that draws across it—
though the curtains close the vision,
though the stranger end his visit,

though the snow erase all traces
of his passing through the village,
though his step become unknowable
and the whiteness knowledge.

FROM *THE SUGAR MILE*

[The East End of London, September 1940]

GRANNY MAY AT THE SCENE

I thought I'd lost you, Joey, who are these
      All over everywhere
      Don't stand and stare
At her she's had a shock, look at her eyes.

Thought you'd joined the navy like your dad
      I did just then I thought
      He's off to war I ought
To stop him he's too young I said I prayed

I weren't too late, I asked the Lord a favour.
      Won't say what I said
      I'd do for Him instead.
Only I'll have to do it now and I'd rather

See your dad come home again. What's done.
      That stretcher's coming out
      That lady's put a sheet
Where someone ought to be and you're too young

To look at it. That house it's disappeared.
        A thing like that can't just
        Happen, Joey, the rest
All spared. Look at his hand, he wasn't spared.

Cover it up, that's right, they must have been
        Spies or something Joe.
        Must have been in the know.
Hitler must have thought they knew his plan.

You don't know anything, do you, Joey? That's good.
        Better safe than sorry.
        The King he's in a fury,
He's hopping mad won't stand for it I heard.

Don't know about madame. Don't know for sure
        She knows it's started, her.
        What's that sound, m'dear,
What's a-rattling me diamond cup and saucer . . .

Let's get away now, Joey, leave 'em be,
        Poor dabs. They didn't know.
        These days you never know
Who's moving in next door, next thing you see

They're carrying 'em out. Look at the sky.
        You say that's what they are
        Them circles way up there
I call them angel circles up so high.

It's got about an inch,
         Until it drops behind
That building. It'll get cooler then
         And I shouldn't mind

If it didn't mean they're late.
         That's what I mean: later.
But it won't be dark for several hours
         It doesn't matter

Whether there's any sunshine.
         I mean there's always sunshine
If you think about it, somewhere
         In the Empire at *some* time.

Did you see in the bog place,
         There are maps on every wall
You can look at while you're sitting there
         Lord of it all.

But they're all obsolete.
         They're worth about the same
As what you're doing in the bucket
         While you look at them.

There's Joey Stone.
        Joey we have to
say goodbye.
Because we've nothing,
        see that zero
in the sky?

No aeroplane
        did that it's too
good to be true.
They're sending us
        away somewhere
we won't have you

delivering
        our paper no one
will at all.
Because it's Nowhere-
        shire because it's
Nowhere Hall.

Will you still bring
        a paper to
the ruins, Joe?
Say you will
        no need to
but say so.

First thing I'm gonna do is swipe a car
and get myself back here. Course I can drive.
It's easy, a girl could do it. An Italian
girl could do it, couldn't you, Joey? First thing.

Second thing, hook up with the Upton gang.
Do a little business, coin a phrase,
waste not want not, dig for victory
blah blah blah. Move up west. Next thing.

Next thing, well. Meet an American starlet.
They have them in their army, not starlets,
females, and their army's going to come,
I heard a rumour, if we're in a hole.

This? This ain't a hole. This school's a hole
but we were just unlucky. Took a hit.
Like Mr Albie Rogers is pretending
happened to his house. And you, Jew-seppy,

what are you, vapour trail? We ain't in a hole.
Our boys'll see off Adolf. If we don't,
the stars of the United States, I tell you,
they're trained and they fight dirty, they're luscious.

SALLY PLAYING PATIENCE

It's even got a cinema,
            the farmers like to go there,
Joey, then they smoke cigars
            they have a film discussion
in a room with velvet fittings.

But what nobody tells them
            as nobody tells anyone
is all the famous actors
            and all the leading ladies
Robby you can think of

have also been escorted
            to the villages selected.
No one's saying much about it,
            Joey, but these stars
in costumes and disguises

could pass us on the meadow
            or you could be hop-picking,
Joey, did you ever
            and next to you right there there's
Merle Oberon, who knows,

Harry, all the West Ham team
            are operating tractors,

people with great talents
        are all to be protected
Julie for the future

so there'll still be the pictures
        to go to when it's over
and cups to play for, Harry,
        and parties and by that time
some of them will know us

you'll stand there with your wine glass
        you don't have to be famous
but they know you, you were there, Joey,
        side by side at harvest
when stars were nothing special.

Julie, in the wheat barns
        at midnight when the work's done
anyone could stand there
        meaning what you hope's
their meaning. When it's over

everyone who went there
        will have this bond forever
and we'll bring our children out there
        in cars with silver streamlines
for the grand reunion dancing.

Toffee Mile more like. I saw these lads
with chisels coming back, it makes no sense
the way they look, they're coming back with spades
and chisels coming back
                  and their bloody hands

are black from what on earth is that I go
and Gibb from Beckton says the Sugar Mile
is burning, boys and girls, the world's aglow
this Gibb from Beckton says
                  with Tate and Lyle's

finest dark selection. I say right,
has anyone told the police? But by the time
the words are out they're words to be laughed at
Has anyone tewld the police
                  habout this hawful crame!

I let them pass right by, I keep my cool.
There's hundreds walking out of Silvertown
and someone said they're headed for a school.
Hundreds walking out
                  in shock from Silvertown

today have you heard anything? You've not.
I want some toffee too with my Jenny near me.
Sun has the nerve to shine and with no hat.
I want dark toffee too.
                  No one can hear me.

THE OLD LAD

I close my eyes and see them waving cloths they found.
Rags and things a thousand feet above the ground.

Making calls they made and saying words they said.
Here comes a girl in red to be the girl in red.

There go the men in shirts. I will not focus in
on any face again and, as I focus in,

arms stretch out as if *There goes the superstar!*
I go on trying for years to not know who they are.

Looked for ways to cope with coping with this shit.
Woke up at four, damned if I hadn't hit on it.

Smiled about it, thing my skull has always done.
Got in step with the old lad, got in unison.

Felt the soft foam falling from a rigid prow,
gainsaying all there is: *Now don't you worry now.*

Couldn't believe I'd cracked it, like the wide-eyed folk
who think all strangers function as a spy-network

making the stuff that makes the papers. Smiled a smile
beyond belief in presidential-spokesman style.

Ran back and forth a century from ape to ape
to seek what's *not* okay by so sincere a gape . . .

Okay the neighbour's starving and okay he's here.
Okay a billion times the bit we gave last year

let's funnel into rubbish-bags and tie the ties.
Okay the trains are pulling out and full of eyes.

Okay to sport a badge, okay to wave a cloth.
Okay some went forever and some won't sod off.

Okay the ones like Cheney, whom you mustn't name
and spoil the poem, do the motherfucking same

as ever, and okay the poles to north and south
are vowels: meat and drink and sex to the one mouth

of the only lad, no worries. It is not a smile
that makes you ache. It won't be over in a while

like mine, but I keep trying. Here it comes again,
and now I'm going to die one day and don't care when,

why, with whom, or who remembers what I did.
The smile is wide and smaller only than the lid.

Do it in turbulence as well, I'm a total mess,
but beaming like a stewardess at the stewardess,

who learned to do it years ago from her old bones,
and can do it hissing info into hidden phones

when the time comes. I fly the blue Atlantic sky
in my last century and yours and by and by

my eyes are holes, my heart is air, my knuckles shine.
Only God controls the fasten-seatbelt sign.

It's all He does. I turn a frail page of grey
and all the news that's fit to print this Saturday

is printed there this Saturday. The news that's not,
the old lad's grinning over in a book he's got.

He's pointing out what's funny and it's everything.
We're starting our descent and I am done with him.

FORTY FORTY

History covered its eyes and counted the way
      kids count: getting faster
then slowing to halves, quarters, sixteenths
      but nonetheless faster,

faster in words but slower and slower to reach
      like Zeno's arrow,
though finally all the way to some fat figure
      ending in zero.

Then History turned and blinked: right there
      stood a boy by a hedgerow,
holding his hands to his eyes and saying
      I'm coming to get you!

And his confidence in a game he had
      quite misunderstood
was awful to see and if History didn't correct him
      others would,

so History ventured slowly towards him
      and—I don't know how—
very gently took little hands in big hands and said
      hide now.

A PLAY OF THE WORD

Something was done and she ran from a town
and I'm glad it was done or she wouldn't have come,
but she wouldn't have gone and she's long gone now,
so I'm wondering why and remembering how.

Her hair was the various colours of leaves
in the fall in a heap as we watched her asleep
and we stood there like words with the ink still wet,
as reminders of something she'd likely forget,

or read in the morning and scrunch in a ball.
Her eyes were so wide that they had a seaside
and a faraway sail in one eye then the other
till I envied my brother and I've not got a brother.

Her mouth had this shape that it made and you can't,
we tried it all week and our lower lips ached
as we pointed this out and she didn't know how
she was doing it. I'm sort of doing it now.

Her hands were so delicate delicate things
were careful with them and the length of her arm
was an hour when I saw it at rest on a sill
with a twig in its hand that's in my hand still.

Her body was everything nobody knew
and discussed in the dark till it wasn't that dark
but her feet were so callused they made it clear
We two will be getting her out of here.

Something was done and she ran from a town
and I'm glad it was done or she wouldn't have come,
but she wouldn't have gone and she's long gone now,
so I'm wondering why and remembering how.

You all have your tales and we too have a tale
in the form of a play that we do in the day,
it's a play of the Lord, it's a play of the Word:
if it had to be written it has to be heard.

And we opened the barn for the costumes and sets
that have always been there and the dust on the air
would set us all sneezing and telling old jokes
of old times and old shows in old years with old folks.

And one was the Maker and one was the Man,
and one was the Angel and one was the Stranger,
and all the old lines were as fresh as cold beer
in a morning in March in that field over there.

But she was so puzzled her mouth did that thing
and her eyes were a mist and her hand was a fist
that she held to her chin till our play was complete.
Then she started to laugh. She was right by that gate.

It isn't for laughter we play in our show.
It's not at all funny. It isn't for money,
it isn't for love. But she laughed and her eyes
were the fog as it shrugs in the face of sunrise,

and her ribs were the sea in the shirt she wore:
we were sickened to follow its suck and its swell,
she was out of our reach, she had always been,
but that was our choice, if you see what I mean.

Something was done and she ran from a town
and I'm glad it was done or she wouldn't have come,
but she wouldn't have gone and she's long gone now,
so I'm wondering why and remembering how.

Why are you laughing, we wanted to say,
till one of us did and we wanted to hide,
and her glistening eyes had no answer to that,
so we waited like birds for her swallowing throat

to be still and it was, and she stared at the ground
like a book of her own to be counted upon.
Everything here is made out of card.
Take light from the World and you're left with the Word

which she seemed to be trying to show in the dust
as we crowded to see and could never agree
what she said after that—that our Maker was sick
of his Word? That our souls could be drawn with a stick?

That our Man was a rainbow, our Angel should hang?
Or the other way round? But which ever way round
there was nothing to do but the next thing we did,
which was take it in turns to repeat what she said

having tiptoed unnoticed away on our own
to the elders and olders who had to be told
what a creature she was and how little she knew
and how hard she was laughing and what we should do.

But I was among the ones crowding her light
so her shadow was gone but I wasn't the one
who asked her to tell us what *should* have been done,
in a voice with arms folded and uniform on.

Something was done and she ran from a town
and I'm glad it was done or she wouldn't have come,
but she wouldn't have gone and she's long gone now,
so I'm wondering why and remembering how.

And he asked her to say what the Maker *would* say
and a few ran away. I did not run away
but I want to have done, so I sit on this gate
where there's nothing to wait for at all and I wait.

And she looked at who'd said it and looked at who'd not
and she stood and she started to speak from her heart
what the Maker would say. I can say this to you.
For who lives in this shell of a town but we two?

The elders assembled like stones in a boat
but it sailed as it could, while it could, when it could,
and then I saw nothing and now I see all
and I wait and there's nothing to wait for at all.

And the wind caught the fire with the last of its strength,
the fire they began for what had to be done,
but the fire caught the town and it burned in my eyes
till my eyes were the desert an hour from sunrise.

And I talk of we two, but it's me on this gate,
with an echo of wind when the song has an end,
but the wind didn't do what I too didn't do,
and we won't breathe a word till there's reason to.

ONE THOUSAND NIGHTS

AND COUNTING

I love her stories but they're all alike.
         I don't mean that.
And I'd only dare to think it on my break
and all I get to do on that
is piss this platinum——eat your heart out, Midas——
         until I'm done
and trot like only tyrants trot
quick-quick in case I miss one.

Litre or two to go. Now when I say
         they're all alike
I only mean——I mean in a good way——
that she has certain themes (I'm like
a literary prof these days!) and they,
         what's the word,
recur: Aleppo, Baghdad, Cairo,
wherever the story's set

it's all the same shebang, but this last one
         better not end,
dear, for that rosy glint on the horizon
is only something being sharpened . . .

Where was I? I was training a critic's eye
          on common themes—
as all my thunder starts to trickle—
I'm only like all storms,

all storms are just like me. Theme Number One:
          the djinn: the djinn
I love, don't get me wrong—without the djinn
you might as well read magazines
or lists!—but must they always come in jars
          and rise as smoke
so horribly I can't see any light
for one great swell of muck?

I only ask. I'm reaching for the soap.
          I can hear from here
the clearing of her little throat, the clap
of olive hands—it's just not fair
I'm who I am! I was the master here!
          I mean I am,
and anyway, I've points to make,
a Second Theme. Ahem:

the chambers underground. There are always chambers
          some innocent
tradesman goes about his day and wanders
into by some accident
and bingo, X has lost an eye, hey presto
          Y lies dead,

and treasure's everywhere, but cursed,
and stuff goes really bad—

I'm drying my hands as quickly as I can,
        dear (I call her),
but not before I mention that a man
can dream, yes, in sound and colour
dreams are free, yet in your little tales,
        Peculiar Soul,
they all come true—the smoke comes true,
revenge in a deep hole,

men without eyes and djinn with nothing but,
        a sot who dreams
he'll rule the world and lifts it off a plate
one morning, men in dog-forms
who begged to differ, dogs in man-forms
        who knows why?
She doesn't know, she's calling me
by *name* now! What if I

just stayed here in these echoey cool halls
        forever, free
of stories, free of her, among the smells
of lavender and lime and me,
the free will of the water? That can't be,
        for who but I
can end it, when she shuts the book
at dawn and meets my eye

and I meet hers? Nobody, that's who,
        when our eyes meet,
(her eyes so green) I will know what to do,
when the extraordinary book is shut
and her fingers touch each other. Till that day
        I am content
to hear her poor preposterous tales
of how the old world went.

FLAGS AND CANDLES

Flags line up an hour before they're chosen,
wave back along the row at others like them.
Candles sit in boxes or lie still,

sealed, and each imagines what will happen.
Flags will not accept the explanation
of why they were not needed as they are now.

Candles feel they're made of stuff that's soft
for a good cause, though maybe not their own cause.
Tall flags love all flags if it's their flags.

Small flags are okay about immense flags.
Candles doze in xylophones of colour,
thrilled their purpose may be merely pattern.

Flags are picked out one by one. The others
muster in the gap and say *Gap, what gap?*
Candles dream of something that will change them,

that is the making of and death of candles.
Flags don't dream of anything but more flags.
The wind is blowing; only the landscape changes.

Candles have the ghost of an idea
exactly what the wick is for: they hope so.
Flags have learned you can't see flags at nighttime,

no way, not even giants in a windstorm.
Candles learn that they may do their damnedest
and go unnoticed even by old candles.

When I wave flags, flags think it's the world waving
while flags are holding fast. When I light candles,
candles hold the breath that if it came

would kill them; then we tremble like our shadows.
Flags know nothing but they thump all morning.
Candles shed a light and burn to darkness.

RENDITION

It was quiet in their zone. They liked to call it
The Zone, it gave it borders.
But it gave the quiet an edge, it gave the quiet
a hum, more like a drone,

more like an engine coming through so they called it
Home. Then it went quiet.
Would you look at that, they said. They called all things
things that made them quiet.

They found a man so quiet what he knew
was everything there was to.
He was quiet when he was asked why was he quiet.
And he was asked why was he

LOUD when he was LOUD and he was LOUD
for 97 seconds.
Why are you loud, they said, you were so quiet.
He answered in both forms.

Why is it dark again, they said, it was light.
Why is there Guns N' Roses
playing, it was not. Why does this light-stick
leak, do you think it's busted?

THE TINSEL MAN

What with the year we'd had it was in the air
to ditch that holiday but the thing is old,
       it's always held,
so it isn't up to us and to be fair
       the children like it.

So we prised the coffin-box and the cold breeze
was all our yesteryears, while on the road
       by the wayside
the man himself was spotted, his big face
       not understanding.

That days arrive as dates is not a thing
he gets, so to be hoisted shoulder-high
       hip hip hooray
and to be crowned with tinsel in the morning
       sunshine was something!

And we laughed into the town, at the great fools
we were again, and we took his weight in turns,
       we wrote new lines
for age-old melodies, we banged the bells
       in our tradition.

And he was fed before he had a chance
to ask to be, and had his pick of girls
            and was all smiles
but didn't pick and they just stroked his hands
            as he stared at us.

Who knows if he remembers this is what
we do with him? Who knows if he believes
            the town behaves
the same way every day? Who gives a shit
            is another thing.

And another thing is timing. It was noon,
then it was after noon, and the white sky
            so recently
blue in his brain was white so he gripped his throne
            and with his language

fought to stop it leaving him. His words
were belted out so loud they meant one sound
            till that one sound
meant nothing. He was focused on some clouds,
            then other clouds.

Mime was all. We think what he meant was *Fight,*
They Are Everywhere, They Are Coming! But the sun
            blushed the maroon
the girls had worn and was gone from there. It was night
            and he didn't stop

wailing till the dawn came and the sun rose.
We leave him to his Morning Victory March
   to the near edge
of the wood as he sheds his terrible old clothes
  and decorations.

MANDELSTAM

Knowing no word of his I embrace his every
word. They're all there is. He died for only
them. I imagine the obstinate syllables
of his name like a bothering hand on the lapels
of Stalin now and then. I imagine him
having it brushed away. Neither of them
strikes me as caring greatly about the dull
ache the other makes elsewhere in his skull,
not even when those closest to them come
wondering *What are you going to do about him?*

Only a slow accrual of discomfort
can do it, and only at night at a point where hurt
and thought converge and clarify the future
with nothing but new words, whether a line
begun forever or one jotted sentence.

ELEMENT IT HAS

It may not be the same, what we appear
to thrive or slow or fade in, though across
its white expanses steadily we stare;

the only common element it has
is loss, and it may differ in the terms
it gives it. And it thickens with the days,

thins in the night as if it more than seems
a carbon thing, afflicted, prone to what?
To us, as if obscurely hopes or harms

can come to it, as if it walks the street
in love, abashed, abused—as if it, too,
expands to wonder at the point of it—

contracts to desperation in the blue
morning, helplessly expands anew.

DUST AND FLOWERS

Everyone ever was shuddering past
In a rubbishy cyclone of them and the dust
And my eyes were attempting to follow some face
I would lose in a blur like a chariot-race

So I'd try that again, and to anyone seeing
I seemed to be one who was stuck disagreeing
And shaking my head sort of slowly forever
Like somebody chronically stupid or clever,

When *you* broke the surface between it and me,
And you stood there as quiet as Sunday will be
While we're having a Saturday—I was the same
For no time at all, till your face and your frame

Were nodding my head up and down on its stem
Like a flower in the rain at the height of a storm,
But afterwards too, like a flower in a breeze,
And always, which doesn't have flower-similes.

ANYTHING BUT THE CASE

Do me my elegy now, or I'll scrawl the thing
I scrawl as you're going or screw in a ball when you're gone,
Or you and I write unaware in each other's tongue
That you or I ever set foot . . . Or do what our son
And/or little daughter got done: got our brilliant names
Pricily grooved in marble by one skilled
In times of loss; dream iridescent dreams
It's that first Saturday. Let this hour be filled
With anything but the case, so that Time the clerk
Goes panting in horror from gremlin to error to glitch
And his screen is stripes and he knows he saved his work
In one of a billion files but fuck knows which,
And he lets us alone or, at worst, as we tiptoe by,
Feels we're familiar, can't for the world say why.

EMPIRE STATE

Departed I could see her
from my new room in Manhattan—
loneliest of letters
in the tallest word in English.

It's like she'd crept alongside,
a great bejewelled someone
at the dark edge of a party
we could not stand any longer.

And still at the wide window
we considered making contact,
she haplessly three-coloured
and I knowing all about that,

but we settled for the vista
through the traffic to the water.
Since *nothing lasts forever*
was about all I could muster.

KASPAR HAUSER

My dream of her
was memories in heaps and the whole morning
at her age now

I think of her
is memories in heaps. In the great daylight
I do nothing

but see stars
like the wolf-boy they sat down in a world
of nonsense.

I can't remember if this happened yet
but the King came in and cleared out all his pals and sat
with everything akimbo and said *Do the bit
where I love you, little señorita, cut to it.*

So I told him what had happened, I mean hadn't yet,
and it was the longest time this man had ever sat
for anything. He roared *I now believe that bit!*
He wanted astonishment from me so I went for it.

I asked him if he'd got round to believing yet
that he'd be slaughtered where he stood. *Or where I sat?*
he chuckled, and I sat corrected. *Just a bit,*
he murmured, *I'm the King, of course I'll swing for it . . .*

But I'm going to free you, girl! I wouldn't do that yet,
I said, and someone came and served us as we sat
in lovely sunlight, then he dozed a little bit,
so I said, Your wife will kill you. He said, *Go for it*

mine angel. I do know, but didn't quite know yet
if that meant her or me. My little black cat sat
on Agamemnon's lap and bathed himself a bit.
She'll kill you in your bath. *Will you join me in it?*

he giggled. You will love me, sir, I said, and yet
you'll never have me. (This is the last time we sat
face-to-face.) 'Cause you won't get it up. He bit
his nails and stood. *You gypsy bitch you don't know shit.*

HOMETOWN MYSTERY CYCLE

FOR CLAIRE MESSUD AND JAMES WOOD

But I was one of the children told
they play the Creation on Applecroft Road
while Abel is battered on Barleycroft Lane
and if I go with him he'll cop it again

at the top of Old Drive. If I stay with the Ark
I'll have seen a good twenty-one Floods before dark,
but I know the place well as the front of my hand
so I watch it in zigzag and still understand.

The dawn's coming up over Handside Green
as Hell's being harrowed by Christ in sunscreen,
but another one rising by pulley-and-rope
at the corner of Mannicotts isn't the bloke

who Thomas is gaping at over his eggs
on a little white trestle on wobbly legs
by the scout hut on Guessens. The stone's rolled away
as slowly as you can roll papier-mâché,

and Judas is keeping his anorak zipped
as he checks on his lines in a ragged old script.
Pilate is bicycling by. If we're quick
we can leg it to Lazarus, set up our picnic,

still be in time for the beauty they've got to
assault with tomatoes till Jesus says not to.
Over the chimneys we hear as we hurry
the loudspeaker crackle the usual story

about a lost child, and we chuckle and say
You'll be late to an angel we pass on the way.
We hop all the hedges of Attimore Street,
where a girl who got rid of me rinses His feet,

and it's too much to take so I plod to the pool,
for the Slaughter of half my old nursery school,
but they lie there and giggle, they're clearly okay,
to the fury of someone who's 'Herod today

and John tomorrow' I joke to my mates
but they've spotted the Virgin in wraparound shades,
and we pass the Three Wise Men, muddled by props
in the shade of an alleyway down by the shops.

Afternoon tires of us, everyone tires;
I hang around people who hang around fires;
three mothers attempt to look vaguely surprised
He is striding already up Mandeville Rise;

but the little girl chosen Star-Girl for the day—
Has anyone seen her?—the drunken PA
is trying to be serious and nobody has.
The imbecile doing Balaam and his Ass

is playing for laughs so he's not getting any.
Judgment is here, they've unloaded already.
Satan is making a meal of a yawn.
We rush up to God *Hey we saw you at dawn!*

So how's the day been? and, to illustrate how,
He ploughs an old finger across an old brow
and puffs out His cheeks like we might blow away
but we don't understand so we nod and we stay;

we are gravely observing the fools in their cart,
then they go and it's quiet and He says *Can we start?*
to nobody really. Just one more to go,
but we've ticked every box so we've seen every show

and it's chaos again as it is every year
with the carts in a ditch and *Whose bloody idea*
was this in the first place? somebody bawls
in the queue for the luminous-necklace stalls,

but he can't really mean it, he has paper wings
his daughters deface with embarrassing things;
he's played about every last role in the Cycle
(he'd never been Michael but now he's been Michael)

and someone is holding a ladder that trembles
and someone has wound a great zero of cables
around his strong arm, and he stares in my eyes
as I say *Weren't you Peter?* which yes he denies

and someone is binding the Cross to a Jeep
and someone is bearing a burden asleep
with a garland of foil and a cellophane star,
who, in other versions, is found in a bar

and in at least one is found stabbed in a pit.
You know your own villages: write your own shit.
I've never done much and I didn't do this,
but you asked where I come from and that's where it is.

THINKING: EARTH

So I was thinking: *Earth*.
And I was earthed as any poet is
by the word alone in its own empty space.
Earth. How the word begins
      with force, as breath

begins and its vowel lasts
as dreams do—or the pauses between numbers—
for as long as the brain can take it. How it closes
as the tongue steps to the teeth,
      presses and rests

till the air is gone. *Earth*.
Seen only in its spot by pilots strapped
for oxygen, their exhalations trapped
inside a crystal ball,
      some ghost of myth

foreshadowed in a scribble
on a cave-wall. My garden's going south
by sixty miles a year, and the caught breath
of botanists—as strains
      mutate, redouble—

itself would power a mill
when they next gasp. Between twin hegemons
of ice and sand we wait, where the mindful seasons,
autumntime, springtime,
      lie down a while,

old exiled diplomats
whose answers were too intricate, too rich
for the liking of the tsar. Now on the edge
of deserts they endure
      odd tête-à-têtes.

*

I fly above the earth
today, dreaming a moment when I'm old,
though living one undreamed-of as a child,
a sliver of pure luck,
      freedom, health,

statistically safe,
and yet aghast and tethered by the fibres
to everything. We'll chat to our dead forebears,
drawn to the life, on screens,
      soon enough.

On we fly until,
brilliant and sleepy between meals,
we come to land on islands green as apples.
We chat on the horizon's
      infinity-pool.

At night on jet-black screens,
if, as we slither back in our own choosing,
we accidentally click on Channel Nothing,
we might just spot through crackle
            of descending lines

what seems to be foul liquid
spreading over sand, but we're aware
was taken from ten miles in the air,
and is a million people
            run ragged.

                    *

Earth. I have a daughter.
Heaven's what I say it is for her.
Telling her is all it is so far
for me. My only use
        for the word *forever*

is in those conversations.
Earth, I think we farmed that word from you
and now can't seem to make the damn thing grow
anywhere, for patience
            tries our patience.

That number on Times Square
plummets upward, digits to the right
are dim with speed. But the one on the far side
is locked at nil, as if
            it thinks we're there.

Graphs that all their lives
ran up and down like children now outreach
a lonely tentacle that leaves the page
to grope for something warm
       where nothing lives.

And it's been forty years,
eyeball to eyeball with the way we look,
blue and alone, bulb of a child awake,
wondering No, but *what's*
       behind the stars?

That casts me into space,
her father, the one opposite, old bloke
propped against a pillow on the dark,
helpless in the face of
       her helpless face,

while, home on earth again,
scientists are furrowing their brows
so deep they are thought fools by folk who raise
hosannas to the sky
       for Superman.

IT TOO REMAINS

You've gone. I mean *you're* gone. You didn't
        have a say.
I don't believe you're anywhere and
        while they pray

I picture you. The images push
        forward one
to stand for all the rest, and when that's
        sort of done

a voice arrives, a tone of voice, a
        certain note
I almost hear, can almost manage
        in this throat.

And as of now that's that and all I
        feel is true
is you're at peace. Whatever soul they're
        chanting to

once had a face and voice I gave it
        and it too
remains at peace, only it's now at
        peace with you.

DREAM-I-BELIEVE

Dream-I-Believe I brought
        out of the night still streaming
                out *It was real I was right!*

Dream present still I could still
        believe in, if I twisted
                likelihood to serve it . . .

Dream that was gone I mourned
        and quoted, sought and lingered
                on sections to my liking.

Dream I had had depended
        on puns, events, encounters
                even to come to mind now.

I seemed to have held four faiths
        by breakfast, and I'd packed them
                fighting to their buses.

So I could sit exhausted,
        stretching in the sunbeams
                like my mother in the old days.

A WALK BY THE NEVA

While the river gathers the many folds of its gown,
        rises to sit and turns to stone,
the figureheads
        on the rostral columns break out into brides

married in just a moment at the prow
        of Vasilyesky Island. So
the city sails
        in time: the buildings glide in parallels,

the giant dreams his dreams of Holland. Peter's
        work is always done and never,
never quite,
        as another bridal party bustles into light

and the long white limos wait with their small bouquets,
        still as the marble case after case
of every tsar
        in the sharp fortress on the farther shore.

The widest flow flows to a point, and here
        there's you, in a crumpled suit somewhere,
picking me out
        of the line as a poet, there's you on a party night

with your beautiful new bride *This is my wife,*
        Mr Maxwell—the fact is, Joseph,
I didn't know,
        I thought you were having a laugh with a bloke and so

I stopped a waitress and said *By the way here's mine.*
        There's a castle of drained pints in London
was it Highgate?
        Hours of talk I don't forget and do forget,

as the widest flow flows to a point. And here
        I am, where you are never. The air
flutters the last
        bride of the morning. I am the Wedding Guest

at we all know which wedding, always about
        to follow the congregation out
into sunlight,
        but held by something at the garden gate

until the lawn's deserted and it's dark.
        When will it ever be fucking dark
in the month of June
        in this town of yours? Never, and pretty soon.

The limo driver's grinding a spotless shoe
        on his dead cigarette and I knew you,
that's all.
        The bride is impatiently at the beck and call

of a cameraman. The tiles of the river are old
        snapshots, silver and brown and curled,
moving and still,
        rustling into the east, into the equal.

CASSANDRA

You. I won't foresee for you one thing.
You staring into space, you moulding creatures.

You thinking if you stop it then the world ends.
Little old you, it does. Mine doesn't, yours will.

But I won't foresee for you, you won't believe me.
You rub your eyes and write. You've not believed

life's anything but a grin into the mist
for some time now, although you gasp at line-breaks

like something spoke to you. O it spoke to you.
I'm at your window now: I breathe the year

you'll leave on the warm glass. Beyond my wild hair
blossoms the to-come but you're so distracted,

you, by lips, by ways, you think like me—
wake with one face a sniff away forever,

speak the lines she speaks at the moment she
speaks these you speak and set your lips where she does,

then you'll see nothing coming or becoming,
and all will be so well.—It will be well,

but I won't let you hear that. If you hear it
you won't believe it, there's where our curses meet

like kisses. All will be well. You didn't hear it,
you, therefore believe it, as your fingers

whittle at the keys to the bright screen,
as the windowpane goes cold and I move on,

trespassing away down your lawn,
over the wall and out across farmland.

9 780374 533496